WITHDRAWN
A Quick Start Guide to
SOCIAL MEDIA MARKETING

**High-impact, low-cost
marketing that works**

Neil Richardson,
Ruth Gosnay and
Angela Carroll

First published in Great Britain and the United States in 2010 by Kogan Page Limited

120 Pentonville Road	525 South 4th Street, #241	4737/23 Ansari Road
London N1 9JN	Philadelphia PA 19147	Daryaganj
United Kingdom	USA	New Delhi 110002
www.koganpage.com		India

© Neil Richardson, Ruth Gosnay and Angela Carroll, 2010

ISBN   978 0 7494 5758 7
E-ISBN   978 0 7494 6192 8

British Library Cataloguing-in-Publication Data

A CIP record for this book is available from the British Library.

Library of Congress Cataloging-in-Publication Data

Richardson, Neil.
   A quick start guide to social media marketing : high-impact, low-cost marketing that works / Neil Richardson, Ruth M Gosnay, Angela Carroll.
      p. cm.
   ISBN 978-0-7494-5758-7 — ISBN 978-0-7494-6192-8 (ebook)   1. Internet marketing.   2. Social media–Economic aspects.   3. Online social networks–Economic aspects.   I. Gosnay, Ruth.   II. Carroll, Angela.   III. Title.
   HF5415.1265.R526 2010
   658.8'72—dc22
                                                                    2010013997

Typeset by Graphicraft Limited, Hong Kong
Printed and bound in India by Replika Press Pvt Ltd

CONTENTS

10 Questions answered 130

PREFACE

In good times or bad, it is important to understand marketing's role and how it can be used by businesses to improve their competitive advantage. Marketing communication in the digital world is vitally important as it's concerned with creating relationships and promoting mutual value. That said, with busy, fast-paced lives, professionals often find that they don't have time to trawl through weighty, traditional texts in order to get to grips with the basics. Hence *A Quick Start Guide to Social Media Marketing* is a user-friendly guide aimed at business people for whom implementation is the key issue; however, it is also useful for students who want to grasp the fundamentals. Each chapter has a summary, some questions for you to consider and some activities to help you apply what we've discussed to your company. Answers to the questions and guidance for the activities are in the final chapter, as is a Glossary, which we hope you'll find useful.

If your websites are to stand out among the millions of worldwide websites they must achieve brand awareness. Brand awareness relates to how well potential buyers can recognize or remember your brand compared to others in the same product category. To achieve this you may strive to build brand awareness, increasing the visibility and accessibility of your products by building alliances and networks. The networking nature of the electronic media makes it easier for your company to use collaborations to gain improved market access, reputation endorsement or simply added mutual values.

The internet and digital media have changed the fundamentals of marketing. The digital age has increased the power of consumers when making purchasing decisions, meaning firms must adopt a more customer centric approach. Digitalization has not only benefited the consumers, but also the companies. It has given them greater access to markets they would not have conventionally aimed at and has helped reduce their costs.

The text outlines the key concepts and principles that govern the subject of marketing communications in the digital and interactive age with particular emphasis on the key area of social networking. It also gives key insights into how theories and tools work in actual business scenarios; it shows how to use social networking, and other digital marketing communication tools, to improve customer satisfaction, which is the ultimate goal for all business people; it also highlights contemporary issues, such as sustainable communications in the 21st century.

Finally, may we take this opportunity to thank you for buying this book. Having bought it you are now one of our customers, which means a lot to us. As you progress through the chapters you'll see the theme of customers being the single most important stakeholder in a marketer's professional life. We have considerable experience of teaching across the whole range of ages, industrial experiences, organizational types and markets. When we're teaching Chartered Institute of Marketing (CIM) students we're often asked a diverse range of questions. We've encapsulated these questions in this text and offered honest, sometimes critical answers. The CIM students are professionals studying in their spare time and they are truly representative of the whole spectrum of companies involved in marketing. Hence this text is aimed at all types and sizes of organizations, large or small, new or old, profit making or charity.

CHAPTER 1
A CHANGING LANDSCAPE

The goal of any marketing activity is the cultivation of, and communication with, targeted prospects and customers. So how does this apply in the ever-changing world of e-marketing? The first step to answering this question is to appreciate what e-marketing actually is.

E-MARKETING – HOW CAN IT HELP YOUR BUSINESS?

E-marketing involves more than simply having a website and it's more than likely that you're already using many of the tools for successful e-marketing. It can help you to achieve a number of your key objectives, namely, to attract new customers, strengthen existing customer relationships, reinforce brands and enhance loyalty. It can help create a fundamental shift in business and customer/consumer interactions similar to that associated with the introduction of automobiles and telephones, ie it has changed the way goods and services are taken to market.

E-marketing, using the internet as a platform, allows you to adapt to the needs of your customers (which is absolutely crucial in today's business world!). It will help to reduce your transaction costs; it gives customers the freedom to buy goods and services any time, any place, anywhere. It involves using your existing and emerging communication and data networks to impart personalized and uninterrupted communications between you and your customers and (arguably) provides value above traditional networks. Importantly, it allows you to easily communicate key details to your customers; for example if you change your trading hours, you can get the word out efficiently and effectively.

Social networking

A quick trawl through most generic marketing texts will produce very little in terms of Social Network (hereafter SN) sites. So why concentrate on SN sites? Well, simply put it's deemed by many to be the marketing channel with the most impact for you and your business in the short- and medium-term future. SN sites enable you to:

1 build profiles with differing degrees of privacy in your internal systems, eg intranet;

2 generate user lists with whom your staff can make contact; and

3 gain access to user-generated contact lists made by others within your systems.

Since their introduction, sites such as Facebook, LinkedIn and Twitter have attracted millions of users, many of whom use these on a daily basis. Undoubtedly, more and more marketers are looking at online SN sites as places to advertise to a targeted audience because with hundreds of such sites and millions of users worldwide, the growth of social networking is phenomenal and is the effective way to target and communicate with the online community.

A changing landscape

Any manager who has been working in business over the last 10 years has undoubtedly seen a great deal of change. Whether it's the changing marketplace, customer needs or tumultuous economic conditions, one thing is a certainty: technology has been central to driving much of the change forward. If you consider how technology has changed your own life, you'll appreciate how it has infiltrated the very essence of your daily activities, increasing the pace of life and providing greater choices than ever before.

In the UK, young consumers tend to spend more time online than watching TV. Also, thousands of home users are switching to broadband each week. Hence, with billions online globally it's easy to see the long-term potential for e-marketing. The advance of these new technologies has brought about a revolution in marketing communications (hereafter marcomms) that affects your company and more importantly your customers.

In the domain of 'marcomms', technology has been at the forefront of much of the development. In our bid to secure customers who are becoming more technologically adept (and some may argue more fickle) technology:

- enables communicating in an interactive manner;
- stimulates two-way conversations;
- creates awareness and enlightenment in a crowded and cluttered environment;
- allows us to create and develop more sophisticated approaches to communication.

From traditional marcomms such as TV advertising, sales promotional activity and public relations, technology has spurred us forward to use and embrace concepts such as flash mobbing, viral seeding and of course... social networking.

That said, to be able to use contemporary marcomms activities, particularly social networking, it is necessary to understand how communication works at a basic level. Once this is understood, you'll have the foundations needed to build understanding and skill with regard to developing your marketing and communication activities on social networking sites.

FAQ: SO, HOW DOES 'MARCOMMS' ACTUALLY WORK?

You would think that the above question would be relatively simple to answer. However, as with most things in life and particularly in business, understanding how marcomms works is actually more complex than most people initially believe.

Over the years, marcomms activities have increased in importance and have become a central activity in most people's lives. Whether we are the people who create and send messages to the marketplace or the people who receive and react to them, it's fair to say that marcomm activities are part and parcel of our daily lives. So, let's try to answer the above question.

First, we have a sender who is the person or organization that is creating the communication or message. The message is sent via a medium or media, which is the means through how they get their message to the receiver. The medium could be a newspaper, magazine or indeed a SN

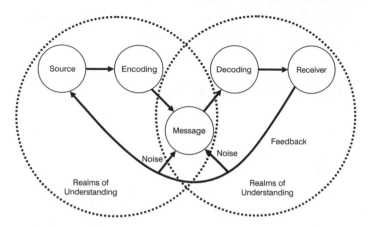

FIGURE 1.1 Linear model of communications. Based on Schramm (1955) and Shannon and Weaver (1962) as cited in Fill (2009, p 42)

site. The receiver quite simply is the intended target for the message. Easy isn't it? However, we can be a little more sophisticated than that. If we really understand the nature and habits of our receiver we can 'encode' the message that we are sending to them.

Simply put, all encoding means is that we can dress the message with signs, symbols and language that the receiver will completely understand. To do this effectively you need to truly understand your target audience. For example, if you are choosing the medium of SN to communicate, do you know enough about your target audience's lifestyle, interests, what will capture 'their' attention, etc? One of the reasons for failed communication activities is the failure to encode the message correctly, so think about how you intend to present your message.

Hopefully, the receiver will be able to decode (ie understand and interpret) the message and respond accordingly. However, there is something you need to be very careful of when creating and sending your messages and this 'something' is usually referred to as 'noise'.

FAQ: WHAT IS 'NOISE'?

Noise can be the curse of a communicator's life. It's with us every day and all around us and it can interfere with the basic communication process.

The easiest way to explain noise is through a quick exercise. Most of you at some point yesterday probably watched TV or read a newspaper or magazine or even spent time on a SN site such as Facebook or Twitter. Write down in the next 10 seconds the last advert you saw. What was the brand? What was the central message they were trying to communicate? Don't just remember a particular advert you've seen recently; write down the actual last advert you saw before going to bed last night... Struggling? You're not alone. It's an exercise that most people tend to struggle with. Why can't you remember? After all, the people responsible for creating and sending these ads have probably spent hundreds of thousands of pounds (if not millions!!) trying to reach you and spent weeks (even months!!) creating and preparing the ads.

Why can't you remember the ad?

The reason you can't easily remember the last ad is often due to 'noise'. This can be information overload – we are so busy with work, cooking, cleaning the house, doing the school run, etc we can only take in so much information. We are bombarded with information today, not just in our daily working lives but with marcomms messages and we simply can't remember everything we see or are told. Even simple things like whether we are in a good or bad mood can affect what we see and how much we take in, what we notice and, more worryingly, what we don't. Technology has certainly exacerbated the amount of 'clutter' in the environment. Next time you switch your computer on and log onto the internet, try to actually notice the amount of marcomms messages being sent to you.

SN sites provide opportunities for you to communicate on a massive scale with different audiences. Currently, young British people spend more time on SN sites than anyone else in Europe, with 25 per cent spending an average of 5.3 hours a month logged onto websites such as Facebook or MySpace. Moreover, sites like Facebook allow you to create pages that your client and suppliers can contribute to and it wants marketers to make more use of the sites (Hemsley, 2008).

While recognizing that SN sites provide access to the elusive youth audience, there's evidence that people of all walks of life use SN. Hence the nature and language needs to change on a site-by-site basis. In other words you must tailor your language to your target audience or your message will simply be lost amid the noise.

Therefore, an additional skill and task of a good communicator is to be realistic and understand the nature of noise and create marcomms that can cut through the clutter that's bombarding us today, to be the key piece of communication that our receivers actually notice, remember and respond to. There are many ways to do this, for example we can use techniques such as using music.

Nostalgia isn't what it used to be!!

Ruth writes 'Growing up throughout the 80s, whenever I have the TV on and I'm reading a book or magazine, one thing that does make me look up and look at the TV screen is if I hear a tune from this era. Animation, fantasy, imagery, music and sexuality are all instruments we can use to help create attention to our piece of communication.' Think about the marcomms that have captured your attention lately – why do you like them? What draws your attention to them? What is it about them that makes you notice them above all others? Is there a generational feel to your nostalgic longings? Can you tap into this when promoting your company?

FAQ: WHY IS IT A PROCESS?

What we also need to remember about marcomms is that it isn't linear, it's a continual process. Why? Well, quite simply because as the world and marketplace is continually evolving around us and our target audience and receivers are changing around us, so do our marcomms activities. Our messages need updating and, as stated earlier, technology has had a profound effect on this area of marketing. The nature and means of how we get our message to our receiver has never been more exciting with the options we now have available. Using SN sites as a channel to communicate is a relatively new phenomenon, as is the use of blogs, wikis and flash mobbing (discussed in more detail in Chapter 6) when compared to traditional forms of media such as TV or cinema. But although there is the excitement and choice, there is also challenge.

Therefore, whenever we create marcomms, whether it is a piece of PR, a sales promotion, an ad or direct mail letter, etc, we must always create a mechanism that allows us to monitor, control and check whether the communication has worked and achieved its objectives. Using contemporary approaches to communication is no exception. We often spend large amounts of time and money on our marcomms activities so we need to know if they are being effective or not. If they are... great!! But why have we got it so right? What can we take from this success to create another? If we have got it wrong... why? Is it the message that isn't clear? Is it the media we've chosen to carry the message to the receiver that is wrong? Is it down to noise? Is the encoding ineffective? We need to know quickly if the communication is not working and to investigate why so we don't make the same mistake twice.

MARCOMMS IN THE REAL WORLD

What you will also notice (see Figure 2.1) is that the communication process doesn't exist in isolation from the outside world. Wider external factors such as socio-cultural factors, economic, political and legal factors, among others, are always moving and challenging the marketplace, businesses and indeed the customer. Consider the relatively recent rules on what we can and cannot advertise to children. Another example is that of the packaging of cigarettes. Legislation can be devised and implemented that can affect our marcomms activities. The downturn in the UK economy in 2008/09 certainly affected many business decisions, including those on communication. Many organizations cut expenditure during hard times particularly on their marcomms activities that are deemed to be expensive, such as advertising. However, the reverse should actually be the case. The environment can certainly affect your marcomms activities – this shall be explored in the next chapter.

When marcomms work well they can provide untold success for your brand/company, etc. However, if they go wrong, they can have quite devastating effects. Not only can precious time, money and resources be wasted, but also brand names, brand equity (the value of the brand) and the reputation of the company can all seriously be affected adversely. Because many of our marcomms activities are highly visible, our mistakes are there for all to see... including our intended receivers, our competitors and the media.

FAQ: HOW CAN WE BE MORE SOPHISTICATED?

Hopefully, you've found the basic process of communication relatively easy to follow. As you now have a basic understanding of the process, we can start to build upon it even more. You need to be practical and realistic if you wish to be a good communicator. One of the key factors to take on board quickly is that, despite understanding how the communication process works, there are inevitably many influences upon it and none are more important than the people who surround us every day.

Therefore, we need to acknowledge and remember this when we are creating, planning and executing our marcomms activities whether they are traditional or contemporary.

FAQ: WHAT IS AN OPINION LEADER AND AN OPINION FORMER?

The terms 'opinion formers' and 'opinion leaders' are what many practitioners refer to when considering the communication process and the influence certain persons can have upon it.

An opinion former is somebody who usually through their education and profession has expertise that you listen and respond to. Quite often many companies trying to communicate a new headache or hay fever tablet may use a chemist or doctor in their communication. Why? Because the use of an expert in their field builds trust and credibility into their communication activities and brand – they are using an opinion former.

Alternatively, an opinion leader is somebody who through reasons such as their social standing, closeness to us generally or just general credibility, we listen to.

Remember when you are creating your marcomms activities, sometimes you're not only intending your message to reach the user, but you will also need to draw in and reach others who may support and ultimately influence the purchaser.

If you consider the speed at which SN has taken off – particularly among certain age groups – the use of peers and the strength of word of mouth (or WoM) communications have all contributed to a viral effect that has spread the use of social networking throughout the world. With the recent explosion of Twitter onto the SN scene, one can't help but wonder if the use of Twitter by celebrities has helped it on its way.

FAQ: WHAT ABOUT TWO-WAY COMMUNICATION?

What we have started to see over recent years is the development of more interactive communications, for example what is termed 'many-to-many' (or M2M) communication.

Digital-based technology allows the free flow of conversation without the boundaries of time or space (see Chapter 6). This creates a great opportunity for an organization to communicate on a truly interactive platform particularly with regard to convenience, speed of communication and relationship building. You only have to look at the initial success of YouTube where events include users uploading or contributing their own content as well as viewing other user-generated content.

SN sites provide an array of communication activities for a business. They initially allow users to share their experiences, to communicate with friends and find new ones, developing a new social link in society. Forms of sponsorship, advertising, sales promotion and Public Relations (PR) opportunities (among many others) are still key tools that can be used with this media. Likewise there are a variety of additional tools that are technology-based which can also be used.

By late 2009 there were 150,000 software downloads available for smartphones. Hence the applications or 'apps' that provided search functions became increasingly important. For example, iPhone Arcade is a free app that can be loaded onto SN sites. It allows previews of games and users can rate the games and inform their contacts via Facebook, Twitter and e-mail. It's limited to Apple's App Store, but it helps to illustrate the subtle change in Apple's iPhone marcomms campaigns. The focus shifted from being on the phone itself to the apps. This was also evident for users of Android-based smartphones where Sidebar provides a tailored search function based on rudimentary research questions. Marketers should appreciate these shifts from advertising the product features to the benefits the apps can give to the users.

Advertisers are certainly being attracted to SN sites. With users posting their details on the site, this allows advertisers to build a pretty good picture of them and they are therefore able to 'encode' their messages and target users more precisely. Opportunities for PR, sponsorship and other communication opportunities are also ripe for use.

ISSUES SURROUNDING CONTROL AND SECURITY

Many users are becoming dissatisfied with the amount of 'noise' and 'clutter' starting to appear on SN sites and other such digital media. It has been reported that users are already logging in less to SN sites such as Facebook, Bebo and Twitter and once logged in, are actually spending less time on the sites. Third party companies are increasingly using SN sites to carry out research without the permission of the users. Therefore, although you undoubtedly have some sound opportunities to develop your marcomms via SN sites, there are also inevitable pitfalls, which will be looked at later.

SOCIAL NETWORK USERS AND YOUR BRAND

Michael Nutley, Editor-in-Chief of New Age Media, argues that the success of branded SN sites will depend increasingly on brand strength and the ability to extend the brand. As with traditional marcomms, SN users will need to buy into brand extensions. Dr Martens set up a SN site in 2006 based around music, but New Age Media discovered in 2007 that fewer than 4,000 people actually signed up in a year. Had the brand been stretched too far? Why go to a shoe site to find a music-based community when there are alternatives such as MySpace?

Where there are synergies, you can work with other like-minded organizations to extend your brand. A group of the UK's most famous museums, including the British Museum and the Victoria and Albert Museum, joined together to create a £1.5 million treasury-funded SN site. The site allows users to search easily and quickly across a range of collections and to set up groups and communities.

HOW SOCIAL NETWORK SITES CREATE NEW OPPORTUNITIES

Web 2.0 brought about a step-change in how suppliers and consumers behave. It was effectively a process of 'creative destruction' where a company's traditional marketing abilities and consumer insights were challenged by the new dawn of user-generated content. Web 2.0 has effectively made companies' knowledge bases redundant. They can no longer perceive users and customers in the same way. This has led to new opportunities and in turn unforeseen market growth, for example the aforementioned Apple iPhone apps market. Market boundaries have been redefined as companies have sought to differentiate their campaigns to create and target new segments. New entrants to the enlarged market have had greater freedom and have been more innovative. Consequently, many established companies who have not embraced Web 2.0 innovations such as SN sites, have been left behind.

Apple's iPhone advertising campaigns increasingly push the convergent nature of their product, ie it's a multi-use tool rather than simply a phone. This shift in consumers' perceptions of smartphone usage has serious considerations for other industries and some companies saw opportunities to enter new markets.

In December 2009, online estate agent Rightmove's shares dropped more than 10 per cent in one day when Google announced a potential website for 2010 where estate agents could list properties free of charge. Even the suggestion of such a site was enough to drive Rightmove's shares down.

When Google (the new entrant) announced their iPhone sat nav app in 2009, shares in existing providers fell sharply.

These are just two examples of Web 2.0's creative destruction and it's a challenge for managers and marketers alike.

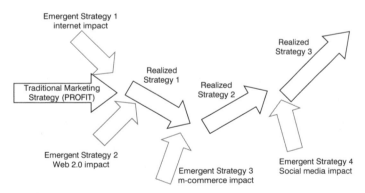

FIGURE 1.2 Traditional marketing strategy being deflected by emergent Web 2.0 factors

Figure 1.2 illustrates how a company's best strategic intentions could be deflected by the failure to adopt or react to

Web 2.0. Many companies have struggled to react to the pace of change due to user-generated content. YouTube has 15 hours of content posted for every minute of the day! This isn't simple growth, it's an explosion of content that reflects many micro and/or macro-environmental changes (to be discussed in Chapter 2).

So, hopefully you now have a good basic understanding of how marcomms work and how many organizations are moving away from the use of traditional media and to the use of the many-to-many media options available and how we can build upon that foundation to become even more sophisticated with the use of truly interactive communications. There are many influences upon the marcomms process including the wider external marketing environment, which we'll now consider.

TOP TIPS

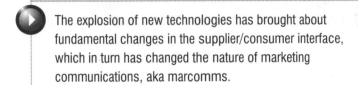

The explosion of new technologies has brought about fundamental changes in the supplier/consumer interface, which in turn has changed the nature of marketing communications, aka marcomms.

The basic communication process involves a sender transmitting a message via media to the intended receiver. The sender can encode the message specifically for the receiver to decode and interpret.

Noise often disrupts the communication process and can result in the message not being received. Noise can be in the form of general information overload; the intended receiver may simply be in a bad mood!

People of influence, whether because of professional expertise or just general credibility, can often affect others. They are therefore often targeted via marcomms activities to create changes in behaviour.

Many-to-many communications, such as social networking, are increasing in importance from a communications point of view. However, although these sites provide additional opportunities, there are the inevitable downfalls to consider.

QUESTIONS

 Explain the following terms: encoding, decoding, noise.

 Why are experts sometimes used in our communication activities?

 What is the difference between an opinion former and an opinion leader?

ACTIVITIES

 Consider a piece of communication from your own organization. Who is the intended receiver? What is the message? How has the message been encoded for the intended receiver?

 Has your organization used any experts/professionals in their communication campaigns? What improvements have they made or alternatively what could they make?

 To see the Museum project visit the following site: http://www.vam.ac.uk/about_va/online_learning/index.html.

 Also, Dave Chaffey's site is worth a mention in dispatches. Have a look at http://www.davechaffey.com.

CHAPTER 2
THE
ENVIRONMENTS

As can be seen from Figure 1.1, the communication process sits well and truly in the wider marketing environment. This means that the wider macro variables that are part of the marketing environment can have a profound effect on your ability to communicate. The marketing environment is split into two parts: the macro environment, which consists of forces that are deemed uncontrollable to a business; and the micro environment, which consists of parties who can be influenced.

We will now focus upon the wider external environment and explore how these forces can affect your communication activities and social networking opportunities.

THE MACRO ENVIRONMENT

The macro environment consists, as stated above, of forces that are completely uncontrollable from a business perspective (Figure 2.1). STEEL PIES can be used to describe the key factors that make up the macro environment... and it's easy to remember! So, what does STEEL PIES stand for?

Social/Cultural Factors

Technological Factors

Economic Factors

Environmental Factors

Legal Factors

Political Factors

Informational Factors

Ethical Factors

Sustainable Factors

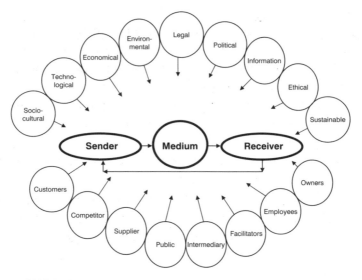

FIGURE 2.1 Communication model with environmental interaction

All of your marcomms efforts are at the mercy of the above forces. They combine to create the macro environment, which is constantly moving and is often fast-paced and volatile. Therefore, you need to constantly monitor them and:

- take advantage of any opportunities that arise

- steer or manoeuvre your business and communication activities clear of any underlying threats.

Social/cultural issues

Society has been evolving over millennia. Lifestyle, hobbies and attitudes have evolved and, naturally, what we deem acceptable in our marcomms activities has changed tremendously. Increasing individual wealth and disposable income have led to new needs and aspirations. Many countries have ageing populations and shrinking youth markets and businesses are adapting their targeting accordingly. Hence your marcomms activities must reflect the current circumstances of society and SN sites are no exception.

Our culture is also evolving. If anything, we feel that the pace of life is quicker than before and the rate of change is accelerating. Remember, when the iPhone was launched it only had 11 apps. Within three years there were over 140,000!! Opportunities are there to be exploited but you need to be quick. Consumers can be fickle and the 'trend' of the moment can be gone very quickly.

Technology and SN communications

Technology continues to develop and converge. This creates opportunities and threats for your business and marcomms activities. SN sites such as MySpace and Facebook can now be accessed via TV sets manufactured by Samsung, Panasonic and Sony. In the UK most of Channel 5's key outputs are shown on YouTube, creating a virtuous circle of converging technologies with SN being Yin to TV's Yan.

With more users accessing SN sites via their mobile or PDA such tools are becoming more important for marcomms. With the arrival of 3G handsets, a new medium has begun to open up through the use of multimedia messaging (MMS) technology. Mobile telecoms companies, eg Vodafone, paid huge sums to acquire the licences and hence actively drove the promotion of text and MMS technologies which in turn increased the traffic on their networks. Some commentators thought that the sums paid for licences (£23 billion in the UK) acted as a serious brake on the development of the 3G market. The forthcoming 4G revolution presents, if anything, even greater opportunities for change and it's to be hoped that the politicians don't kill the golden goose.

Mobile or m-marketing

The Direct Marketing Association defines mobile or m-marketing as 'the process of marketing campaigns delivered via the mobile medium' (DMA website http://www.dma.org.uk/content/home.asp). They go on to say that m-marketing has a number of unique benefits – it is 'always on, always with you and messages are always read'. UK mobile penetration reached over 90 per cent of the population in 2009, which is truly exceptional (ibid). There are four billion mobile phone users worldwide of which 500 million are smartphone users. That said the number of smartphone users is going to increase dramatically!

Adapting your marcomms to allow mobile users to access SN sites allows you to:

- dynamically track user responses, ie in real time;
- respond quickly to events.

When combined with its potential for growth (which some think will outstrip traditional PC-based browsing) 'm-comms' will become a key platform for your organization. No doubt many firms are not preparing adequately for the future m-commerce boom, which is unwise especially as it will play a major, if not dominant role in the future of e-commerce.

Despite the hype surrounding the emergent m-marketing channel, improvements are needed before it reaches its potential. Recent developments (eg Vodaphone removing tariffs for roaming across Europe) mean that the relatively high charges for mobile internet are coming down. Most mobile websites struggle to deliver an effective experience, which is a fundamental problem as ease of use and func-tionality are key to the user experience.

Suffice to say it's essential that you monitor (and are ready to react to) technological changes. Rest assured your competitors will!

Economics and SN sites

As the global economies slowed and world trade fell in 2008–9, the changes provided opportunities and threats to businesses and their marcomms activities. As con-sumer spending and confidence fell, businesses were forced to look at ways to increase their income while continuing to provide customer satisfaction in very effective and efficient ways.

For example, sales promotional activities within digital media were used more frequently as a means to stimulate consumer behaviour and to 'add value' and 'incentivize'.

The content of your marcomms activities and the media you use should be carefully considered. The use of SN sites can be an extremely cost-effective way to communicate with your target market, particularly in times of economic uncertainty.

Environmental impacts on communications

As society in general has evolved to take a greater interest in our environment, stimulated to a great extent by the media and better education, the need for business to consider the environment in a friendly and sustainable manner is important. If you place environmental awareness at the centre of your business activities you may wish to shout about this from a PR perspective.

Green consumers often object to the use of tools such as direct mail because of the waste of paper involved. With the use of digital media, this type of waste is minimal, although there is the need for electricity – obviously! This issue is increasingly important to consumers and will be discussed in more detail in Chapter 8.

Legal concerns

The development and implementation of legislation can seriously affect your marcomms activities and you must have knowledge of current legislation. You must also be aware of legislation that is in the pipeline.

Globally communications industries are subjected to varying degrees of regulation. Sometimes a combination of self-regulation and statutory requirement exists. To a large extent internet-based media operates under its own rules; there is little international law to govern its use or abuse. However, that's not to say that this state will continue. The governments of Europe and the United States are working upon joint legislation to control the internet, but this is easier said than done. How you determine what is and isn't acceptable behaviour when operating across international and cultural boundaries is extremely challenging.

There are varying degrees of control among SN providers – but it isn't law per se. Facebook has been targeted by malicious hackers seeking to steal data from its users. Security is a key issue with regard to SN sites. Whether you are seeking to develop and run your own site or post your messages on others, responsibilities with regard to privacy and security need to be seriously considered. Hackers have the ability to place a virus upon your site and steal saleable data and SN sites are easy targets. The law has not caught up with the development of digitalization; therefore, as a user or owner of a site, you need to be diligent in how you provide security measures to protect both your brand and your users.

Politics and SN sites

Many governments are striving to increase broadband speeds and access to the internet. These political decisions have provided businesses with greater opportunities to target users and convert them to customers. Governments make many policy decisions that in turn can impact upon your current and future marcomms activities. It is governments who create social, economic and environmental policies etc... therefore it is necessary to ensure that you know of these decisions. That said, some governments aren't comfortable with the open nature of social media such as blogs, fora and SN sites. Famously, Google had a stand-off with the Chinese Government over the issue of censorship and dissemination of political messages.

Informational issues and SN sites

The need for information from a business point of view is crucial. Information provides the basis of effective decision making and therefore its availability and content accuracy is an issue. Digital media have created dramatically improved access to information for the global audience. SN sites can provide:

- your own branded site to pass key information and communications to your users;
- a platform for your marcomms, ie on somebody else's site;
- access to user-generated information from blogs, price comparison sites, public fora, and other SN sites.

You can learn a lot from social media users via the comments and conversations they have. This will help you to encode and tailor your messages to them more accurately than ever before, targeting potential customers with greater precision. However, there are ethical implications, which we'll discuss now.

Ethical issues and SN sites

As stated throughout, the ethical issues surrounding social networking media are very prevalent. Privacy campaigners are concerned about the implications of the data and information that can be found on SN sites. They worry about the potential for organizations to use it in an 'unethical' manner, for commercial and profitable purposes.

But herein lies the issue – what is considered ethical or unethical? It is a grey area for any communication or marketing work and will be discussed in more detail in Chapter 8. The need for ethical behaviour is paramount as we are venturing into what is often regarded as unchartered territory. So use sound judgement.

FAQ: What about sustainability?

You can find all you need to know in Chapter 8.

Environmental surveillance

Now you should have a better understanding of the need to constantly scan and survey the wider marketing environment. There are opportunities and threats for your company; however, you must be able to react quickly. Environmental scanning is the term often used to describe the systems used to survey the changing environment on a regular basis. It can be undertaken by:

- reading key newspapers and magazines such as *The Economist*, *Media Week*;
- watching the news;
- liaising and networking throughout your business community;
- reading industry, government and market intelligence reports (eg Mintel, Datamonitor, etc).

Ensure you organize yourself and your resources and systems for effective scanning. In the world of social networking the environment is often turbulent, volatile and fast changing.

THE MICRO ENVIRONMENT

The micro environment (Figure 2.1, page 20) involves those stakeholders in and around your company over whom you have some influence. As the world changes, so do the stakeholders with whom you interact. Every change can have a knock-on effect on what, and how, you communicate. The degree of influence you can exert varies from stakeholder to stakeholder. You have the most influence over your staff and (with SN sites) the least over the users. We'll come back to customers throughout the book and particularly in Chapter 3.

TOP TIPS

The macro/external environment is uncontrollable and must be continually surveyed to identify potential opportunities and threats.

The STEEL PIES framework identifies the forces of the external environment that require monitoring (socio-cultural, technological, economic, environmental, legal, political, information, ethical, sustainability).

Environmental surveillance is required to try to keep abreast of the ongoing changes in the environment that can potentially affect social networking opportunities and threats.

ACTIVITIES

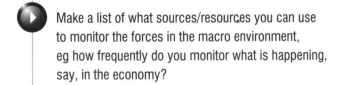

List the variables in the macro environment that you need to monitor.

Make a list of what sources/resources you can use to monitor the forces in the macro environment, eg how frequently do you monitor what is happening, say, in the economy?

Start tracking some of the communication messages on social networking sites. It may give you an idea of how content and use of tools differ over time and circumstance.

CHAPTER 3
USERS AND/OR CUSTOMERS?

All companies seeking to market themselves via SN sites face fundamental challenges regarding 'identity'. Who are the 'users'? Are users and buyers the same thing? Can you treat users of Twitter in the same way as you would Facebook or LinkedIn?

AN IDENTITY CRISIS?

There are major differences in the reasons why and how people use different SN sites. Some may be light-hearted, eg Facebook or YouTube, whereas others may be more professional, eg LinkedIn. Indeed, business people are increasingly using SN sites such as LinkedIn as part of their online research activities. Hence you need to co-ordinate your marcomms activities to be able to address different communities and networks accordingly. These factors need to be considered because ultimately you're trying to change their behaviour by influencing their decision-making process.

Identity

The issue of identity needs to be considered closely as SN sites feature networks and communities who share values.

You'll not always be able to identify your prospects and users/buyers. This makes the act of segmentation much harder as users of MySpace, Facebook, Twitter, Bebo and other SN sites tend to put their best face forward – a practice known as disaggregation. Also, the use of multiple identities on SN sites has become the norm. Have no doubt: users' identities are multifaceted, fluid and often deceptive.

Despite this it is still worth persevering as our 'spending' is shaped by our thoughts, feelings and the actions of those around us. We adopt the attitudes, beliefs, opinions and values of our family, friends, communities, colleagues, reference groups, opinion leaders and so on. With SN sites new forms of identity are being shaped by networks and communities.

THE DARK SIDE OF SOCIAL NETWORK SITES

A challenge for those seeking to market to users and prospects on SN comes from the ethically dubious practice of identity theft. ID or personality theft is a growing practice and a MySpace search in early 2008 discovered more than 700 comments accusing others of stealing from their online personalities – avatars, favourite songs, witty remarks, background designs, even entire profiles.

CASE STUDY

Fraser and Dutter (2008) refer to a site called FriendFlood which, for a fee, posted messages from attractive 'friends' on users' profiles to create the impression that they, like their friends, were attractive and fascinating. FakeYourSpace brazenly offers to 'turn cyberlosers into social magnets' by populating users' walls with physically attractive 'friends'. The site ran into legal problems after complaints that it was using photographs of fashion models from iStockPhoto.com without permission.

Such practices are thankfully in the minority and most consumers are ethical and increasingly discerning about such practices. That said, they expect much more than just the core product benefits when purchasing online. Users expect quality service, reliability, personalization, easy use and fun. No one is saying that price is not an issue for consumers but it is rarely THE issue in decision making, hence you need to consider how you can influence them in the right direction, ie your company.

THE DECISION MAKING UNIT

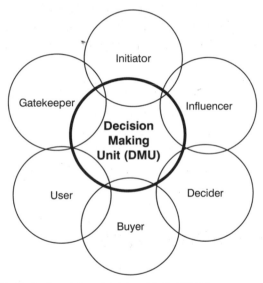

FIGURE 3.1 Decision Making Unit (DMU)

Traditional marketing has always advocated awareness of the Decision Making Unit or DMU (see Figure 3.1); however, it can only be a stepping-off point for SN marketing. The problem with the DMU as a model is that passivity is implied. In small businesses different stakeholders can have different scenarios, eg initiator and user but not buyer. With SN sites the concept of the DMU still applies as different stakeholders will fulfil differing roles while contributing to the online debates. However, it is further complicated by the use of multiple media channels and the stakeholders who act this way are known as multi-taskers.

> Differentiation (by support and quality) is particularly relevant on eBay where hosts of sellers offer identical products with little 'price' differentiation. Users reflect on the seller's reputation as the unethical practice of artificially raising prices with false bidders is a major concern. That said, the economic downturn of 2008/09 saw further pressure on sellers to offer lower prices as reduced user disposable income increased the motivation to acquire cheaper products.

When not in recession or economic hard times non-price factors play increasingly important roles. In fact, if you differentiate your products and goods sufficiently you may even increase online prices as buyers will often pay more to deal with suppliers of good reputation, delivering on promises and support.

BUYERS AND SELLERS

Typically, online buyers are young, employed and have disposable income. That said, you'd be wise to be inclusive and seek to attract people from all segments of the market. Interestingly, over half of eBay's buyers are over 45 and the silver surfers (ie those over 55) are increasingly visible online. eBay also attracts a wide variety of sellers. Originally, sellers were consumers selling unwanted goods to other consumers in a classic C2C sense (Figure 3.2).

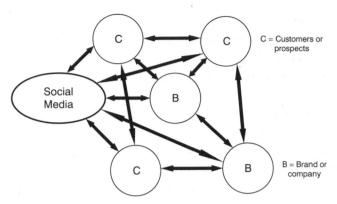

FIGURE 3.2 Many-to-many model of communications in social media. Adapted from Fill (2009)

However, in recent years businesses have begun to use eBay to sell their goods to consumers and other businesses. C2C sales have always been the predominant structure of sales on eBay, but there has been substantial growth in B2C and B2B sales, with B2B sales growing faster than C2C.

SN sites offer opportunities for companies selling to the public and specific communities therein. It doesn't have to be high tech – Unilever was cited as having 231,093 friends of Marmite on Facebook in mid-2009. It can't be established whether such groups actually increase sales; however, having the site provides an alternative to the traditional 'push' form of marketing. In the ideal world you want customers and prospects to come to you and ask about the launch of new products. This 'pull' form of communication is rare (when did you last queue for a new product or ring a manufacturer?) so anything you can do to promote customer demand is worth exploring.

COMMUNITY

The concept of community is crucial to many SN sites and user-generated fora. Pierre Omidyar of eBay said the 'real value and the real power at eBay is the community, we are different because of the way we interact with our community, lose that and we lose everything'. This sense of community has been evident in eBay since its 1995 launch; however, as previously stated it is the advent of Web 2.0 that has raised the importance of 'community' in e-marketing.

Simply put, SN communities exist and it makes sense for you to interact with them and seek input from them. Remember, constructive customer criticism is always welcome as any improvements can only make you more competitive. On a positive note, customers can become advocates, which we'll discuss in more detail in Chapter 4.

AFFILIATES

Affiliate marketing can be an attractive option as it can bring prospects to your site. It's defined as 'a commission-based arrangement where referring sites (publishers) receive a commission on sales or leads by merchants (retailers)' (Chaffey, 2010). Amazon was one of the earliest adopters of affiliate marketing. They launched their Associates Program in 1996 and the US site now has over 4 million pages, many of which will be affiliates who drive visitors to Amazon through links in return for commission on products sold.

How does it work?

Affiliate marketing is often thought to apply solely to e-retailers where the affiliate is paid if there is a purchase on the merchant site. In fact, payment can occur for any action that is recorded on the destination site through a 'thank you' post-transaction page. Companies like eBay and Amazon use their affiliation with, say, price comparison sites such as Kelkoo. The affiliation introduces potential consumers who may not have considered eBay or Amazon prior to seeing them on the affiliate site. This could be a quote for your service or the subsequent supply of a product.

A visit to an affiliate site results in a click-through to your site, which is monitored by tracking software. If agreed actions occur on your site, a commission fee is paid to the affiliate. It's flexible, relatively low risk to you and, importantly, can tap into the growing trend for loyalty cards such as Nectar and voucher sites such as Myvouchercodes or Mirrorcashback. As always check out the fine print and as long as all parties benefit (which is often the case) you could see growth in customer acquisition.

MULTI-TASKERS

In the real world people are increasingly media multi-taskers, ie they can be accessing multiple media platforms, eg TV, online (say Twitter) and mobile simultaneously. Media multi-taskers buy more online compared with those who don't and worryingly for brand managers they are more discerning and hence likely to switch brands after online research.

The number of multi-taskers has increased by 38 per cent since 2006 (EIAA, 2009) with 22 per cent watching TV while going online simultaneously at least once a week. The demographic is not restricted to the young, with silver surfers (ie those over 55 years old) seeing a 75 per cent increase in multi-tasking since 2006. Their willingness to 'change mind' after online research is product dependent with a much higher tendency to switch holidays or FMCG products while remaining loyal to big ticket items such as cars.

Hence with word-of-mouse spreading via SN sites particularly quickly, it's more important than ever to manage your reputation online. The following summarizes the EIAA's tips:

- Socialize campaigns – users are increasingly using multiple SN sites for differing reasons, eg Facebook, Twitter for personal use and LinkedIn or Smarta for business purposes. Hence you must think creatively and combine invention with relevance in your communications. The battle now is for content AND style.

- Location, location, location – mobile devices are driving improvements in m-commerce. The new 4G handsets will drive this even faster and multi-taskers can no longer be assumed to be at a fixed point.

- Timing can be everything – multi-taskers are inclined to go online in the evening. Factor this into your promotional campaigns and be aware of how their use of media is evolving – SN sites are evolving at ever-increasing rates and the environment is more varied than ever before.

- Communicate to convert – multi-taskers are heavily influenced by word-of-mouse – ignore their comments at your peril. You must monitor the micro environment, particularly how others are using SN sites – be aware of how your company is being represented and discussed online and strive to manage this more effectively (see Chapter 2). Also monitor the macro environment continuously – multi-taskers are into the latest technologies hence you need to keep abreast of new developments and further convergence.

THE DECISION-MAKING PROCESS

Traditionally, marketing campaigns encouraged customers to buy products and/or services, ie they sought to close the deal. Marketers too often simply listed features of the product. Pre Web 2.0 this may have been enough to satisfy customers, but these days customers are seeking information on benefits and they're quite happy to enjoy themselves while at it. The thrill of the auction is a key element of eBay's business model.

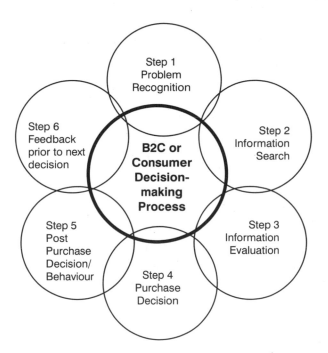

FIGURE 3.3 Consumer or B2C Decision-making Process

However, the advent of SN has shifted the emphasis to helping consumers to make decisions prior to the purchasing decision itself. It's as basic as this – are you now engaged in trying to sell what you think they want? Or is it a case of finding out what information consumers need to make better decisions? If you're too focused on trying to close the deal you could be in trouble. Figure 3.3 shows the traditional B2C decision-making process and illustrates how SN sites, blogs and other user-generated tools now impact on consumer decisions.

SOCIAL NETWORK MARKETING AND SMES

It's worth considering using SN marketing to sell to SMEs even though they have traditionally lagged larger companies in terms of e-marketing adoption. This trend is now changing with increasing numbers of SMEs ordering supplies online and also selling. The UK has 2.5 million enterprises of which 98 per cent are small-to-medium size enterprises (SMEs) employing less than 50 people.

The B2B decision-making process (Figure 3.4) applies to SMEs even though most marketing texts concentrate on larger organizations. However, marketing within small firms is different from marketing in larger organizations. SMEs tend to adopt the characteristics of owner/managers and tend to be more intuitive. This lends itself well to SN sites such as LinkedIn. Some barriers to SME adoption of e-commerce do exist, such as:

- SMEs lack awareness in terms of sources of assistance, eg grants;
- they perceive IT skills problems as barriers;
- they feel their company size is too small to benefit;
- they perceive the required technology to be too expensive/complicated or incompatible with in-house systems.

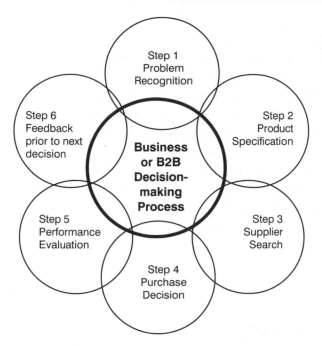

FIGURE 3.4 Business or B2B Decision-making Process

Try to anticipate these issues when marketing your company to SMEs. It's not always easy finding out information, as was proven during a discussion at the Academy of Marketing conference. A room full of esteemed and distinguished marketing academics (who between them have written dozens of different titles) expressed concern regarding discussing the latest Web 2.0 tools, eg Twitter, in their texts. Their concern was that things move so fast that by the time a text is published the tool may have become passé. This attitude is too product-oriented when what is needed is a more customer-centric approach. The tools are indeed changing but a constant is that customers need to know the benefits of what you offer them. This never changes!

CASE STUDY

'Sign-up.to' is a tool that is designed to facilitate easier communications with your customers and target prospects. It can help you to develop innovative personalized relationships. Their database can include a wide range of information about the consumer, which can be updated at any time by the user. Whenever it is updated, all member company databases are immediately updated, so consumers don't need to remember to change their details with every company they are subscribed to. This promotes cross selling across member companies and moreover enables you to develop your customer relationship management by generating more customer feedback.

TOP TIPS

People are the integral part of e-marketing, with the consumer in more control of variables than ever before. In order for you to be successful in your marketing strategies it is crucial that you listen to what consumers are saying and actively encourage their participation in the process. They're no longer passive and waiting for you to promote your brand.

An organization should be both inward and externally focused to truly understand and react to changing customer needs and trends. Remember that the customer should be at the heart of all business and marketing decisions and activities. Providing your customers with what they require by anticipating their needs and satisfying them will entice them to come back time and time again.

Researching who your customer is and what they require is a start to developing a relationship with them. As time moves on, customer needs change and your marketing-related activities need to change with them.

QUESTIONS

 Users of your SN site will almost certainly have multiple identities. How will this affect how you target your customers?

 What are the key benefits that your organization can attain by recognizing the different roles within the DMU?

How has the advent of SN marketing affected the decision-making process?

ACTIVITIES

 Think about your behaviour as a SN user. How have your needs changed as you've grown older? Can you think of any organizations that satisfy your needs really well and whether this encourages you to go back time and time again?

 Compare and contrast the different needs and motivations of the 'actors' in your DMU with one of your customers.

 Have a look at http://www.sign-up.to and reflect on how your company could use such a service.

CHAPTER 4
BUILDING RELATIONSHIPS

The popularity of SN sites is a major issue for 21st-century marketing. Traditional marketing theory suggests that, with hundreds of millions of global sites, your company needs to stand out among the crowd if it is to achieve greater brand awareness and ultimately sales. Successful placement creates (or raises awareness of) your profile while establishing direct links between advertising and sales. Brand awareness is a major issue for many marketers and yet simply improving the ability of a prospect's recall is no longer enough.

Before Web 2.0, buyers had limited options for learning about your services and/or products so you had to raise your brand profile. Largely, this made marketers' jobs easier as they built brands from the top down, starting with mass communication, such as trade advertising and press releases and targeted tactics like direct mail.

In some ways 'push' marketing is straightforward. 'Above the line' methods, ie advertising, can be costly but the overheads are measurable and a return on marketing investment (ROMI) can be established. It's questionable whether SN group sites can replace advertising per se. However, Blake Chandlee (Commercial Director of Facebook) says 'Progressive brands are seeing social networking as an opportunity to connect with customers like never before. When information about a brand comes to you from a friend rather than from a corporation, it gives your brand a completely different level of credibility' (*The Times*, 2009).

WORD OF MOUSE (WoM)

Marketers have always argued that word of mouth is the strongest form of promotion and this has now morphed into word of mouse (WoM) on SN sites. A caveat (to Chandlee's argument about credibility) is that if the brand garners negative publicity the WoM can pass around the world in seconds. You have no option other than to assume that your customers and prospects search online, particularly on SN sites where they can read 'unbiased' peer comments, prior to purchase, hence the top-down approach is increasingly inappropriate. Promoting your company via SN sites can contribute, with good WoM, to a personalized 'pull' method, where users are encouraged to take an active role.

CASE STUDY

In early 2009 Innocent Smoothies sold a 20 per cent shareholding to Coca-Cola and sparked a SN-inspired media storm. For 10 years as an independent manufacturer Innocent received largely positive reviews due to its environmental and ethical practices such as using organic materials and donating profits to charity. This positive brand equity didn't prevent hundreds of negative comments being posted on Innocent's website. The owners were simply seeking growth and economies of scale; however, the association with 'big business' tarnished Innocent in the eyes of some consumers. While supplying hundreds of thousands of customers Innocent was unlikely to 'partner' any large company without upsetting some of its clientele.

It's a cliché (but true nonetheless) that you can't keep all of the people happy all of the time. Certainly the power of blogs and SN sites shouldn't be overstated; however, when in tandem with other media such as newspapers, the resulting fallout needs to be managed. Innocent wrote to its customers stating, 'We will be the same people making the same products in the same way. Everything that Innocent stands for remains in place.'

It's too soon to say if this joint venture will be a success; however, it's unlikely that Coca-Cola would back Innocent without believing that it has growth potential in the European market. Also consider that in mid-2009 Coca Cola had nearly 2 million fans on its own SN site; hence, assuming these communities interact, more people could buy Innocent's ethical, environmentally friendly products than would have done and larger donations could be made to charity. These things are rarely black and white.

FAQ: DO THE BASIC LAWS OF MARKETING STILL APPLY?

As discussed in Chapter 2, the advent of Web 2.0 (featuring consumer-generated tools such as SN sites and blogs) has changed how marketing fundamentals are applied. Increasingly, the power of consumers has grown prior to, and when making, purchasing decisions. Companies must adopt a more customer-centric approach if they wish to 'sell not tell'. It's not all bad as the benefits are not only restricted solely to the consumers, but also exist for your company. Certainly you now have access to markets that may have been beyond your reach with conventional means.

Companies of all sizes can now reach millions of new customers on a global scale that until recently was available only to major corporations. It is the most exciting time there has ever been for starting and growing smaller companies and you can tap into this as long as you recognize that the customers' roles have changed and you need to understand how to add value for customers.

Think about this, many companies are interested in their customers' purchasing habits or preferences and have developed detailed databases to track purchase activities. Yet despite having Customer Relationship Management (CRM) systems and mighty databases the vast majority of new products fail in their first year. Why? Surely the massed ranks of marketers had sufficient customer knowledge to have a better than one in seven chance of surviving the first year. Apparently not!! More than ever before, SN sites provide the opportunity to find out not only what consumers think, but the networks and communities of users, prospects, friends, colleagues and even families.

E-CRM

Chaffey (2010) argues that e-CRM is packed with fundamental common-sense principles; surprisingly, many companies do not adhere to them. Those of us who constantly battle for the forces of good (ie customer centricity) aren't that surprised that many companies misuse their data. Many don't even appreciate the flow of data (see Figure 4.1).

Users of sites such as Facebook generate enormous amounts of data and you'll need to manage the data to produce information effectively and efficiently in order to make knowledgeable decisions, hence CRM programmes

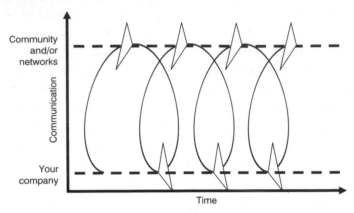

FIGURE **4.1** Healthy dialogue with communities and networks

undoubtedly have something to offer... but they're no substitute for genuine customer insight, which is where knowledge comes in.

It's an old cliché but makes the point well:

Knowledge is knowing that a tomato is a fruit, whereas wisdom is knowing not to put tomatoes in a fruit salad.

Professor Michael Baker (a key figure in UK marketing over the last 30 years) argues that the term CRM is inappropriate. Instead he offers the term (and approach) of Customer Satisfaction Management. CSM is a different mind-set and is not only wholly preferable but lends itself to SN marketing wonderfully. Strive to inspire your staff to do everything in their power to improve the customer experience.

As customers change, their desires, needs, wants and information requirements also change. If your company doesn't change and adapt with them, it's likely that you'll start to dissatisfy customers and lose them to the competition. Hence it's not enough to simply amass a huge database – you have to massage it to ensure the information you extract from the data is good enough to support your decision making and knowledge management.

USING SN SITES TO ACQUIRE CUSTOMERS

You have to make it easy for visitors as there's a high likelihood that non-converts may never be seen again. As previously discussed, SN marketing encourages high levels of customer interaction and collaboration. Once the prospect is on your site, you need to catch their Attention by creating a favourable impression. Using information from their SN site you should have some idea what Interests them. Ensure that your product offer creates some prospect Desire – make it fun or offer free content initially. Then provide the information needed for the prospect to make the right decision, ie take the Action of ordering from your company online.

Always be mindful that satisfaction and loyalty are not necessarily the same thing. Don't overdo the personalization at the cost of ease of use and functionality – a balanced site that appeals to all the targeted users is the best approach.

The next stage is to change first-time customers to repeat customers. Remember it's considerably cheaper selling more to existing customers than it is acquiring new ones. You need to consider your approach for migrating existing customers to online customers (see Figure 4.2). This depends on your starting point, ie whether you offer traditional and/or online provision.

Assume your company has followed the AIDA steps above and entered into the first transaction (ie converted

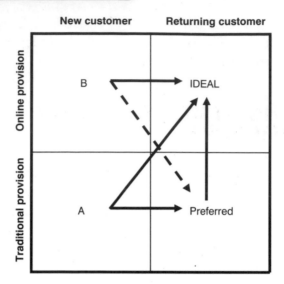

FIGURE 4.2 Approaches for relationship marketing

a prospect into a customer) traditionally (A) or online (B). The first transaction (A or B) is fraught with risks and you must ensure everything is done to 'get it right first time'. Eventually, after they've ordered from you several times, they'll forgive the odd mistake; however, in the early days new customers are easy to drive off. Remember, responding to a mistake says more about your company than when things go smoothly.

Also, not all returning customer positions are equal as your overheads are likely to be considerably lower online. Being pragmatic means having repeat customers in any form is 'Preferred' to single transactions (hence the dashed migration from B to Preferred). Ultimately, whether through single (A or B to Ideal) or multiple migrations (A or B to Preferred to Ideal), you have an opportunity to migrate them to the 'Ideal' position where they're happy to buy online and you enjoy the healthiest margins.

ADDING VALUE – MYTH OR REALITY?

As previously discussed, the concept of 'business-as-usual' is increasingly deemed to be declining and the notion of brands dictating to customers is being replaced by community-oriented engagement marketing. In this scenario a fundamental question that you MUST ask is 'Where is your company adding value?' Is it adding value internally or in the customer's perception (which ultimately is the only 'added value' that means anything)? You may need to consider the key question – who provides the insight? If you get this wrong your company may be pouring substantial funds down the drain. In the case of real-time SN sites such as Twitter this information may evaporate before you've had the chance to act so you may need to change how you monitor the environment.

Life Time Value (LTV)

You're in uncharted territories as one of the new ways of building customer relationships is communicating with (rather than at) them. Your aim is to turn them into satisfied customers and then engage them in building customer communities. You won't be able to control all aspects of the communication process (think herding cats or juggling soot and you won't be far off); however, the benefits to all parties are there to be seen.

The fact that they will want to belong to your community changes the whole dynamic. Dialogue will flow both ways (as per Figure 4.3) with customers, and between customers, to mutual benefit. SN sites like MySpace, Facebook and even Flickr are the perfect forums (or fora if you prefer!) for this dialogue. Many companies do this poorly so you have

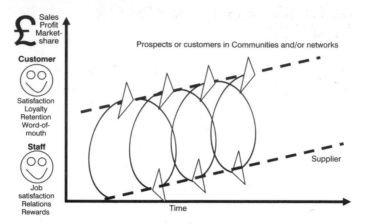

FIGURE 4.3 Flow of information in marketing-oriented company and resulting benefits

what Chaffey (2010) describes as a golden opportunity for integrated CRM to create competitive advantage. Serving and nurturing customers over their lifetime makes sense, as existing customers are, on average, 5 to 10 times more profitable.

Everything you do should be geared up to seeing the customer's Life Time Value or LTV (ie the sum of their contributions to your company over a long timescale) rather than a single transaction.

Say a client spends £100 every other month. Do you treat it as a £100 transaction or as potentially £12,000 over the next 20 years? Every time you interact with the client imagine a figure of £12,000 hangs on the service provision and your whole approach will move towards relationship marketing.

E-LOYALTY

Ellen Reid-Smith is credited with leading the way with much of the early work in e-loyalty. She stresses the need to focus on your most valuable customers, which is akin to Pareto's Law (80 per cent of your profit comes from 20 per cent of your customers... there are other variations) and argues that e-loyalty research can help you to identify your most valuable customers (Reid-Smith, 2009). We can't stress this enough – you MUST be able to identify your most important customers.

Some argue that you can label customers, for example the Boston Matrix refers to Rising Star, Problem Child, Dog and Cash Cow. Such labels are problematic as who is to say that a rising star is worth more or less than a cash cow? In many universities the business schools are Cash Cows as they often contribute heavily to the bottom line. Does this mean you shouldn't sell to them? Of course not!

In B2B selling one of the great buzzes is finding a small account and then developing it into a key account. How do you categorize this? Also these days the marketing environment is moving at such a pace that many of these old tools are too static. Surely your customers mean more to you than a label??

Those of us who have spent many years selling to customers would add that your sales force is an invaluable resource and as a first step ask them the following:

- Who are your most valuable customers now?
- Who will be your most valuable customers in 18 months' time?
- Who will be your most valuable customers in three years' time?

The results should tell you a lot about your strategic direction, not to mention your sales team. These simple questions should inform your e-strategy (as well as your offline strategy). Reid-Smith (2009) suggested a Seven-Step e-Loyalty Consulting Process as follows:

1 Clearly Establish e-Loyalty Goals and Objectives.

2 Identify the Most Valuable Customers (MVCs) and their loyalty drivers.

3 Develop a Strategy to Create an Intelligent Dialogue with Customers.

4 Design a Web offering to fulfil on MVC's loyalty drivers.

5 Formalize an e-Loyalty Program for MVCs.

6 Persuade Customers to Want a Relationship.

7 Develop Feedback and Measurement Tools.

These steps are largely common sense (whatever that is!); however, it has to be noted that theory and practice are not the same thing. The tricky bit is persuading customers to want a relationship, which you can only do with continuous dialogue (Figure 4.1). You must sell the benefits and not simply list the features – sadly this happens far too often. Customers want to know how you can help them to solve their problems. Remember, you're not selling drill bits; rather you're helping customers to drill accurate holes easily and safely which will reduce risk of injury and save them time and money. These are the benefits. Your success will come down to implementing this customer-centric approach and this approach needs support from the top of your organization.

ADVOCATES

Imagine the impact when your customers become advocates for your company. You know when you're really looking after and satisfying your customers when they start 'selling' the benefits of your company to their friends, family and colleagues.

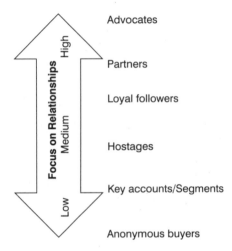

FIGURE 4.4 Relationship marketing continuum. Adapted from Piercy (2009)

Advocates promote your goods and services for no financial gain to themselves. They simply want to share the love!! Would you keep something this good from your friends? When someone you respect and/or care for extols the virtues of a product you'll pay far more attention than if the manufacturer said exactly the same thing. This is what is called non-marketer-dominated communication and is as good as it gets from a marketing perspective.

It's a similar concept to opinion leaders; however, advocates carry even more weight as they've bought your goods with their own money – in other words they've taken the risk. Also they have existing relationships with the people in their community. SN sites provide the perfect breeding grounds for advocacy and as we discussed earlier WoM is incredibly powerful. Your advocates will boost your sales and profits while improving customer attraction and retention not to mention staff morale. Seems too good to be true! Give it a try!

TOP TIPS

 Knowing that word of mouth is one of the strongest forms of communication, the new variant 'word-of-mouse' (WoM) on SN sites is increasingly important. If your company garners negative publicity, the WoM can pass around the world in seconds and you need to be able to monitor and respond efficiently and effectively.

 Customer Satisfaction Management (CSM) is infinitely preferable to Customer Relationship Management. CSM is a different philosophical approach and lends itself to SN marketing wonderfully. As customers change, so do their desires, needs, wants and correspondingly their information requirements. Hence it's not enough to simply amass a huge database – you have to ensure that the information you extract from the data is good enough to support your decision making and knowledge management.

Remember that the customer should be at the heart of all business and marketing decisions and activities. Your organization should be both inward and externally focused to truly understand and react to changing customer needs and trends and recognize that the only place to add value is in how your customers and prospects perceive your company. Researching who your customer is and what they require is a start to developing a relationship with them. Providing your customers with what they require by anticipating their needs and satisfying them will entice them to come back time and time again.

QUESTIONS

How would your company react to negative SN feedback?

Can you think of any organizations that take a long-term approach to their marketing? What sort of SN presence do they have? If none, how would you advise them to improve?

How could you adjust your SN communications to promote the move from short-term transactional selling to longer-term relationship marketing?

ACTIVITIES

In order to ascertain the LTV of your customers, do you know what your key customers want now? In 18 months? Or in 3, 5 or even 10 years? If not... why not?

CHAPTER 5
THE MARKETING COMMUNICATIONS MIX

Most organizations today use a combination of communication tools to achieve their communication objectives. The range of tools available is commonly referred to as 'The Communication Mix' (often abbreviated to the 'comms mix'). The comms mix consists of a varied range of tools that all perform different functions. Some are good at achieving certain objectives, others perform very differently. The big 'six' tools include:

- advertising;
- public relations;
- sales promotion;
- personal selling;
- direct marketing;
- sponsorship.

However, the range of tools does not start and end with the list above. Indeed, as mentioned previously, there are a wide variety of tools available, some of which are shown in Figure 5.1.

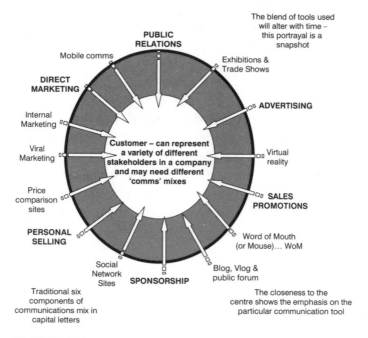

FIGURE 5.1 Expanded communications mix

FAQ: HOW DO YOU SELECT WHICH TOOLS TO USE WHEN COMMUNICATING ON SOCIAL NETWORK SITES?

A good question! Each tool in the mix performs a specific job. This chapter will identify what that job is and how it can be used effectively on your SN. Let's start with what is perhaps the most prolific tool of all... advertising.

ADVERTISING

Advertising is a great tool to achieve a variety of different objectives. It's good at achieving the following:

- awareness;
- educating;
- informing;
- persuading.

As you're aware, advertising can be controversial. It has the ability to draw and tempt audiences to your brand, product and services in sophisticated ways. That said, it can be used in what some may deem 'unethical' ways. But, if used in a considered manner, advertising remains a powerful means of communication. It's a master at drawing attention to (and creating awareness of) new products and services, developments and messages.

The trick is to choose the most appropriate medium (or media if plural) for your adverts. Traditionally speaking, media consists of:

- broadcast media (TV and radio);
- non-broadcast media (print-based media such as newspapers, magazines) or outdoor media (billboards, poster sites at train and bus stations, on taxis etc...).

Today there's a range of digital media at your disposal. Many traditional media owners are struggling against the tide of digital choices: Advertising revenues earned by TV companies, newspapers and magazines are generally falling as opportunities to advertise in more highly targeted digital media options are available... social networking sites being one such option.

Advertising on SN sites creates the opportunity to put your message to a highly targeted market. Advertising is known as a mass communication technique and with the use of SN sites as the media this takes your message to the potential 1.7 billion online users, quite often at a fraction of the cost of traditional media. Whether you are selling advertising space on your own SN site (which is a major revenue stream) or looking to pay for advertising on somebody else's site, you need to be aware of the pitfalls.

FAQ: What are the problems of advertising on SN sites?

As mentioned in earlier chapters, 'noise' and general 'clutter' particularly of advertising on SN sites is becoming an issue, which makes you wonder what it will be like in two or three years' time.

SN advertising is a twist on word of mouth, as the users become virtual ambassadors for commercial brands, often unwittingly. SN sites allow businesses to build custom-designed pages. Users then become fans and any interaction with the brand can then be broadcast to their Facebook friends. This is not a straightforward process as debate rages regarding the effectiveness of banner advertising on SN sites.

> In a recent survey (by CIAO) half of the British internet users never clicked on banner ads. Only 6 per cent said they clicked on banner ads two to three times in a month and just 5 per cent said they do it daily. Other forms of online display advertising were also shunned. Pop-up ads were found to be even less popular than banner ads. Nearly 69 per cent said they had never clicked on pop-ups while less than 3 per cent claimed to click pop-ups daily (Bearne, 2008).

Some argue that banner ads don't work as it is believed that click-through rates on ads tend to be very low, which can result in response rates being well below 1 per cent.

This may be due to 'banner blindness' in which users ignore the areas on the screen usually occupied by banner ads. This phenomenon is well known and it is worth considering that not everyone who sees an ad clicks – this is the halo effect.

Research into the travel market sought responses on the appeal of online ads. It found that more than twice as many people were being driven to a search engine by banner ads than were clicking directly on the banner! This may help to explain the halo effect; however, it doesn't negate the usefulness of banner ads. You may still achieve a decent Return on Marketing Investment (ROMI), but it's crucial that you make banner ads interesting and the better the focus on the target audience the greater the likelihood that you'll see good returns. As always, monitor how other companies, particularly competitors, place their ads online. What is certain is that the use of advertising online and via digital media is set to substantially change the face of the advertising industry.

PUBLIC RELATIONS

Public Relations (aka PR) is a very different tool from advertising. It is generally more subtle and a softer communication tool. This tool is good at:

- building relationships;
- generating and fostering goodwill and trust;
- generating positive stories and conversations;
- developing a long-term positive reputation for the brand and organization;
- countering bad publicity.

If used correctly, PR is often seen to be more credible than advertising as it's not paid for in the same direct way. PR is often a third party endorsement (ie non-marketer dominated) rather than direct from the organization itself (ie marketer dominated). There are many PR activities you can develop to help support your brand and organization.

Much PR is generated through activities such as:

- press releases;
- press conferences;
- media relations;
- event days;
- search engine marketing.

As well as being useful in the external marketplace, PR is also a great internal communication tool. It is also a strong tool to use when trying to counter any negative attention.

As with any of the tools, the digital revolution has not passed PR by; if anything it is being used increasingly online and particularly on SN sites. However, it is a tool that is often supported by offline activity as well. Many brands create activities offline to create a buzz, to get people talking and hopefully enthuse bloggers. Indeed, bloggers are becoming part and parcel of organizations' PR programmes.

Engaging with bloggers in a two-way conversation can be useful to start the viral effect. Controlling the material can be difficult but you can influence it. By studying who is saying what, you can try to maximize the impact. Tracking online PR can be easier than offline PR, which is notoriously difficult to evaluate. You can track the links between a social media release and customers' interaction with your website, etc.

If you have a website presence you can easily hold press releases, company information and product brochures on the site – remember the culture of the younger generations has changed and they now like (or even expect) free content. You need to develop techniques that allow you to enter into relationships with the users who download this information from your site and stimulate two-way conversations, which is where SN sites become useful. Such conversations can only help you with relationship building, as discussed in Chapter 4. Try to avoid having registration online. Remember customers don't have to register when they go into a shop, so why ask them to do it online? If you do insist on pre-registration be ready to cleanse the data – it's amazing how many times Donald Duck has registered with websites!!

Once again though, as with advertising, the ethical boundaries of using PR online and as part of the social media landscape need consideration. The CIPR (Chartered Institute of Public Relations) has developed a set of 'social media guidelines' and encourages the use of the CIPR code of conduct; namely, integrity, competence and confidentiality when considering or using PR in a social media landscape.

SEARCH MARKETING

Search marketing is now a mainstream part of the marketing domain that is increasingly being used in tandem with PR campaigns and direct marketing (which we'll discuss later in this chapter). Not that long ago it may have been seen as something for the 'techies' but now it's a key consideration for marketers and managers of companies of all sizes. Its increased profile is due to being measurable, offering ROMI and also because it links with (and improves) other components of the comms mix.

Current research suggests that search marketing needs to be optimized to work with banner advertising, by anticipating searches that are likely to be prompted by the banner and ensuring a higher rank for your clients' (or prospects') search results. For example, a brand featuring a Cyprus holiday offer will generate generic search terms such as 'package holiday Cyprus' rather than brand searches. Hence search marketing can:

- help to co-ordinate online and offline marketing functions;

- improve transparency across a marketing campaign;

- generate income;

- act as a real-time research tool, eg on SN sites such as Twitter.

Most online customers 'search' using a small number of search engines, namely MSN, Google and Yahoo. Often, people use a search engine site as their home page – a development that has been promoted by the excellent Mozilla. Think of the power this gives to, say, Google. The first brand you see online every day is their search engine.

So if you're seeking to raise your profile (and let's be honest who isn't?) then a great way to get noticed is to get your website listed on these search engines. Some engines are free; however, others involve fees. If you're happy with a (nominal) cost you can buy keywords. But please don't think that simply buying keywords and registering with a few search engines is enough – you still need to be smart. Identify the spending patterns of your target customers and match your search marketing to them.

SALES PROMOTION

Sales promotion is a very different tool from PR. It is often referred to as a 'behavioural' tool as it can truly affect consumers' behaviour. It can add value and induce a quick increase in sales. Sales promotions can be used to:

- increase sales in the short term;
- encourage brand switching;
- encourage trading up;
- encourage trial and use;
- increase frequency and amount purchased;
- even out seasonality if experienced.

The lists above aren't exhaustive but should give you a fair idea of what can be done. There are lots of different sales promotional activities that you can use. What you need to be careful of is the technique you select. The technique you choose needs to fit the objective you wish to attain. The following techniques can be useful:

- Buy one get one free (BOGOF);
- competitions;
- free prize draws;
- trial-sized products;
- money-off vouchers/coupons;
- loyalty cards;
- bulk buying/cash rebates.

FAQ: How can sales promotional activity be used online?

Sales promotion lends itself well to real-time retail activities, for example recent trials were undertaken to enable mobile scanning of bar codes in stores. Labels have limited information and you may not want to ask the store staff such questions, so you would simply use your mobile to scan the bar code and a wealth of information would be instantly available to you.

E-coupons are a particularly useful form of promotional activity that:

- when downloaded can be redeemed online using a code at 'checkout';
- can be printed off and used offline in store;
- can be sent by the retailer to your mobile while instore and may be redeemed immediately.

The hard-copy option poses a problem as coupons can be merely copied and passed around. In some cases this could be a security issue; however, as part of a viral marketing campaign this could be an easy and cheap way to provide a short-term boost to your sales. A tip is to always ensure your coupons have a code to measure the effectiveness and it may be wise to have a time-stamp or 'use-by' limit. You may not want coupons being presented years after the time you were seeking to boost sales.

PERSONAL SELLING

By nature, personal selling is a direct and interactive form of communication – usually on a one-to-one basis that is usually face to face. Personal selling is a great communication tool as it gives the opportunity to speak directly to your customers, suppliers, distributors, etc. Therefore you have some control over delivering the message correctly.

This is probably one area of the comms mix that hasn't been as developed as other communication tools from a technological/online perspective. This will change with the increasing use of video conferencing technology from offices and smartphones used by salespeople. It can improve your sales team's access to customers, particularly those who are remote. Mobile technologies can also enhance the freedom of the sales team, not only to keep in touch with clients while on the move but also to keep in touch with the office.

This tool could prove to be an instrumental part of your communication mix; however, it can be expensive due to its labour-intensive nature. A key point is that the tools in the comms mix can influence each other heavily. Sometimes they can be a constraint, ie advertising can be very expensive. At other times they can energize the other tools, which is the case with personal selling. If you have a sales team it's imperative that they use their interpersonal skills to encourage traditional customers to use your online facilities. Provide incentives so your sales people encourage users to register with your SN sites.

DIRECT MARKETING

Direct marketing, if designed accordingly, is indeed an online interactive communication tool. Database technology is at the base of effective direct marketing. Keeping your stored data cleansed and up to date is key to effective use, and investment and time should be seriously given to this activity. Most people associate direct marketing with 'direct mail', but direct mail isn't the only medium that can be used in a direct manner. Other forms of direct marketing, particularly online, include:

- direct response advertising;
- sales promotion (e-coupons/sampling);
- public relations (blogs and podcasts);
- e-mail;
- viral marketing;
- SMS marketing.

The use of traditional offline direct marketing activities is often used to drive recipients to a website or to phone a particular number where they can obtain the information and help they require. Insurance companies such as Direct Line are perhaps a key example to use here. Watch out for their TV adverts; they usually end with their website address or phone number.

Not all users will want to express their opinions on a public SN platform. Hence give them the option from your SN site to correspond on a more confidential and individual basis via e-mail.

FAQ: What is viral marketing?

Viral marketing uses the internet as a platform to encourage recipients to pass a message onto others. Virals are often humorous, interesting and/or quirky enough to make the receiver feel that there is a need to share it with their friends. Creative content is often key to successful viral marketing. It needs to be sufficiently attractive to get the receiver to open the e-mail, decode the message and respond to it accordingly.

The message may initially be picked up by a few users and 'snowballed' to many via digital means such as e-mail and linking on SN sites. The real-time nature of Twitter has made this site particularly effective for viral campaigns. Users discuss their involvement with products and services with their friends and family through 'Word of Mouse' or WoM (as discussed in Chapter 3). Marketing practitioners acknowledge the potency of WoM and viral marketing is now a key form of WoM. Referring back to Chapter 2, remember, if you want to convey messages to a particular target market you must ensure the content is encoded specifically to them.

Viral marketing can combine being low cost with being highly penetrative and shouldn't be underestimated as it can reach and influence large numbers of consumers and in some cases can then bring issues to the attention of the traditional mass media. We'll discuss viral campaigns in more detail in Chapter 9.

How can Short Messaging Service (SMS) help?

Marketing investment in SMS has increased significantly in recent years. In sending messages directly to mobile phones and PDAs, which can be stored and read later, you have a powerful marcomms tool that directly links you to the customer no matter where they are. Mass SMS marketing is a powerful form of one-to-one marketing that can:

- generate new sales;
- enhance branding; and
- improve your marcomms both internally and externally.

The beauty of SMS is that it is cheap and easy to implement, but the downside is that (with the current technology) the messages have limited content. However, this will change as the new 4G phones become widespread.

Customers may weary of big business invading their space and you should always seek permission before using the SMS channel. SN sites are quick to condemn companies who send spam messages.

CASE STUDY

Amazon has, in many ways, led the way in e-retail and has used SN sites well to provide feedback on texts. However, even it had to change its behaviour due to a viral SN campaign. Amazon chose to label certain books as 'adult' and removed them from searches. This led to an 'amazonfail' hashtag campaign on Twitter. Amazon initially tried to pass this off as a glitch, which led to an explosion of blog posts, online petitions, form letters and protest logos. Have no doubt that how you react to such difficulties often says more about your company than when things run smoothly. Amazon, to its credit, sorted out the glitch and the titles started to reappear.

SPONSORSHIP

Sponsorship is relatively rare (on SN sites); however, it will undoubtedly grow in the future. It links site content with the advertiser and is a useful way to improve your branding and creating or raising awareness. When you sponsor a SN site online, your brand may be associated with that site. Gurgle.com is Mothercare's SN site for new mums and it's feminine, cosy and welcoming (see http://www.gurgle.com/). If this fits with your marcomms and values then it makes sense to seek a sponsorship deal.

TOP TIPS

 E-comms allows you to easily calculate a Return on your Marketing Investment (ROMI). This form of accountability isn't always available with more traditional forms of marketing.

 The communication mix consists of a large number of communication tools. Many organizations today use a combination of tools to communicate their message both online and offline. There are advantages and disadvantages for each key communication tool.

 Using SN sites may allow you to communicate in an interactive, flexible and targeted manner.

QUESTIONS

 What are the advantages and disadvantages of advertising as an effective tool?

 Which sales promotional technique(s) could your company use to promote registrations on your SN site?

 What is viral marketing?

ACTIVITIES

 Consider how virals could drive users to your SN site.

 If you currently don't advertise on SN sites, log onto a site and have a look at the instructions/fees for advertising.

 Consider how you can utilize voucher code sites. Bear in mind that security is an obvious issue where coupons can be merely copied and passed around. Have a look at www.vouchercodes.com.

 For general comms stories have a look at the following:

- www.theindependent.co.uk
- www.brandrepublic.co.uk
- www.brandweek.co.uk
- www.asa.org.uk

 For information on the role of public relations via SN sites look at the CIPR (Chartered Institute of Public Relations) site at www.cipr.co.uk/socialmedia.

CHAPTER 6
CONSUMER-GENERATED MEDIA

SN sites belong to a new and rapidly expanding genre of media called consumer-generated media (CGM). We talked a bit about this in Chapter 4 but let's explore more.

Consumers spend time online sharing their experiences and views of many things in their daily lives. Increasingly, their online activity revolves around discussing brands. This may be in the form of:

- sharing information about particular brands;
- reporting good and bad brand experiences;
- giving their opinion about any aspect of brand activity including advertising and in some cases parodying brand activity.

Not only that, many consumers invite and encourage others to engage in dialogue about these issues, sometimes over a long period of time. Content is frequently archived online for readers' convenience and information.

CUSTOMERS AIN'T WHAT THEY USED TO BE

Since the advent of Web 2.0 CGM has grown quickly and more people have gone beyond merely downloading content and now produce their own material. Online International (Nielsen) currently track over 100 million CGM sources and nearly half of all online consumers have created content (Snol, 2009). Web 2.0 users are deemed to be active rather than passive. The notion of users sitting, waiting for the marketers to inform them of the latest brand innovation was always questionable. Nowadays, users are well informed, often energized or highly motivated and you can tap into this energy.

The expansion of CGM is mirrored in the number of media platforms currently available. Early CGM tended to focus on e-mails, online letters and discussion forums. However, CGM has quickly adopted multimedia techniques and uses the full range of digital techniques and technologies. Figure 6.1 illustrates some of the key forms of CGM.

We will look at some of these in more detail later in the chapter.

CONSUMER GENERATED MEDIA: THE NEW FRONTIER?

We talked in Chapter 1 about 'many-to-many' communications and CGM fulfils this criteria as it involves 'consumer to consumer' (C2C) and 'consumer to brand' interaction. Given the huge growth in this media, this can be a new framework for your marcomms in the digital era (see Figure 3.2 on page 33).

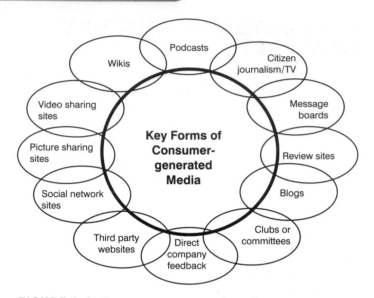

FIGURE 6.1 Consumer-generated media

Consumers, especially younger groups, are increasingly cynical about 'marketer-dominated' communications such as branding and advertising. Companies are increasingly deemed to be less trustworthy and their marcomms are potentially less effective. CGM empowers consumers as the ultimate WoM (word of mouse) vehicle. It is consumers who are in the driving seat leaving sellers to patrol the digital highway. A significant dimension of CGM is the sense of community generated with mutual exchange of information/ideas. The vast majority of online users now regard CGM as the most trustworthy form of recommendation.

So now let's explore some of the key CGM platforms.

Blah, Blah, Blah: Blogs

Like many forms of CGM, blogging rapidly mushroomed from a fringe activity to a mainstream phenomenon. So what actually is a blog? A blog (contraction of the term Web log) is a website, usually maintained by an individual, with regular entries commonly displayed in reverse chronological order.

Traditionally, blogs adopted a diary format with highly personal musings on 'what I did today' often creatively packaged as 'hey you guys, you'll never guess what happened to me today!' Some blogs are also used for the display of visual material such as graphics or video. The collective community of all blogs is known as the blogoshpere. It's a bit like Mars – out there somewhere. The fact that all blogs are, by definition, on the internet means that the blogosphere is interconnected and socially networked.

CASE STUDY

Technorati, the blog search engine, has indexed 133 million blog records since 2002 and estimate that there are approximately 900,000 blog posts in a 24-hour period. However daunting this may seem, you need to monitor comments on blogs regarding your organization and other stakeholders in your micro environment, ie competitors, retailers, suppliers, distributors, agents, etc. Some of the comments will be disproportionately critical – it goes with the territory of anonymity – however, others will provide genuine insights of tremendous value. You can engage with the bloggers in a positive way and, undoubtedly, those who can be seen to listen to consumer feedback and then implement changes will reap the rewards of adopting a more customer-centric approach.

WHO BLOGS?

The blogosphere has been created by many different authors, not just consumers. However, its dynamic nature means that commentary about a company or brand might be picked up and tapped into by a range of people who could be operating in a public and/or personal capacity. Figure 6.2 represents some key blogger groups.

FIGURE 6.2 Key blogger groups

As discussed in Chapter 3, blog users (ie the author and those who respond) can have multiple identities. For example, a marketing professional might be writing one minute about how best to target Yummy Mummys and the next minute ranting about the latest Brand X 4WD gas guzzler.

More recently, the activity of blogging has been glamorized by the advent of Twitter. Although essentially an SN site where people subscribe to 'follow' an individual's entries, authors on Twitter write micro-blogs of up to 140 characters. Celebrity Twitterers such as Demi Moore and Ashton

Kutcher, Stephen Fry and Barack Obama have generated positive publicity for the site and the term blogging.

This self-publishing format has been dubbed the 'my story' phenomenon, which both empowers individuals and bestows authority on the author. The blogging communities (Figure 6.2) have a strong sense of belonging, cultivating relationships and bonds. This fuels the tendency for bloggers to rely on other bloggers for news, information and opinion and to quote and reference each other rather than sources outside the blogosphere.

Some individual bloggers have become recognized as 'experts' on particular issues by virtue of the number of times they are cited by others. The practice of operating in packs means that the influence of self-appointed authorities is not restricted to community members and information and opinion is quickly diffused to a wider public domain as search engines index them. This is particularly true when the word 'problems' is used in the search in connection to a brand. Where there is negative commentary about brands on the internet much of it appears to be blog-generated.

CASE STUDY

A classic example in blogging folklore is known as 'Dell Hell', which whipped up a storm for the computer giant in 2005. Jeff Jarvis, a prominent US blogger and a communications professional, wrote about his faulty Dell laptop and bad experience of Dell customer services on his site Buzzmachine. It was not long before many other dissatisfied customers tuned in and posted their negative experiences of Dell. The story was brought into mainstream coverage by *The Guardian*, the *Wall Street Journal* and the *New York Times*. At the time Buzzmachine was ranked as a key online source for consumers with a negative perception of Dell's customer service and a highly influential voice on Dell customer service in general.

So it's easy to see in the era of CGM why the internet has been dubbed the 'Wild West' by media practitioners.

HERE TODAY GONE TOMORROW?

You'll want to attract new customers (as all businesses lose clients) and then you want to keep them satisfied. Also you want to use a platform that reaches both clients and prospects alike. SN sites offer this in a unique way, but the problem remains which one(s) should you use. It's not just a matter of using what's in vogue now.

CASE STUDY

Twitter was undoubtedly the SN site with the most buzz in 2009, rapidly growing to 10 million global users. The number of UK users rose by 1,900 per cent in 12 months, but is Twitter's popularity enduring? Nielsen Online suggested that in mid-2009 an average of 60 per cent of users failed to return to Twitter after one month. Compounding this further, research from Harvard suggested 90 per cent of its content was generated (in mid-2009) by 10 per cent of its users and that most people only tweet once every 2.5 months. Despite only being two years younger than Facebook, Twitter's user base is dwarfed by Facebook's 200 million users. You need to consider such factors when considering how you wish to target your messages.

VIDEO AND PICTURE SHARING

The recent popularity of visual content creation via the web is perhaps most visible on video sharing sites, with YouTube being the most popular example. Here, individuals can easily upload videos they have made for the world to watch. Topics are wide-ranging, from the mundane to the bizarre.

What is evident, however, is the extent to which some of these homespun efforts capture the public's imagination, with YouTube producing viewing data and a ratings service. It is easy to draw parallels here with the nation's obsession with reality shows such as *X Factor* and *Pop Idol*. Thirst for fame is quite rampant, especially among the younger 'digital native' groups, even if talent is mediocre or lacking completely. There seems to be limited capacity for embarrassment at showcasing these talents to a public and global audience.

Once, such displays would have been kept private – confined to the front room or bedsit. As the new frontier of CGM expands, the desire to be 'out there' has never been greater and support for the outsider is never far away. Witness the volume of hits (27,964,906) for the YouTube video of 47-year-old, unemployed Susan Boyle in the heats of *Britain's Got Talent* in April 2009.

However, YouTube is also an important showcase for advertising. Many commercial adverts are placed on the site. Until recently this could be achieved without declaring it as a 'sponsored' video, and commercial and home productions were often intertwined. Currently YouTube offers a sponsored video service which effectively means that sponsors are identified.

CASE STUDY

A brand that uses video effectively as an advertising medium is T-Mobile. The 'Dance' advert was filmed at Liverpool Street station via a flash mobbing initiative and involves the waiting passengers engaging in seemingly spontaneous dance. To date, it has attracted 13,188,957 hits on YouTube despite the fact that it was also shown on mainstream television. Not bad considering that prime time television programmes on commercial channels are now lucky to get 5 million viewers.

The blending of the commercial and the homespun is evidenced in the number of advertising parodies that are placed on YouTube. Here, individuals make 'mash ups' of regular adverts, mainly aired on TV.

CASE STUDY

An enduring favourite is the techno-mix mash up of the advert for Cillit Bang by Jakazid. This uses a techno soundtrack but features clips of the actual advert with 'Barry Scott' (more of him in Chapter 7). Originally this was show-cased on Jakazid's website but presumably due to popular demand is now on YouTube and has 3,262,723 hits. There is a similar production for esure.com car insurance featuring Michael Winner and the 'calm down dear' strap line.

These two examples make entertaining viewing but other parodies are more amateur and not all attract viewers. Regardless of the quality, all mash ups represent a form of advertising mediation by consumers. This is the Wild West after all and brands are no longer in full control.

Other creative skills of consumers are showcased on picture sharing sites. Billions of pictures have been up-loaded and many are tagged with text descriptions and/or geotagged with the latitude and longitude co-ordinates at which the image was taken. Flickr is one of the most popular picture sites globally. Although individual users of Flickr and similar sites are simply using the site to store and share pictures of their experiences, travels, parties, pets, family, etc some organizations are using these images to create a 'big picture' of how digital natives present themselves.

An analysis by Cornell University, New York of 35 million photographs uploaded on Flickr revealed that the Apple Store in Manhattan is the 5th most photographed place in New York and the 28th most photographed place in the world (Redfern, 2009). A search for 'Apple store' images on Google will therefore link to someone's snaps on Flickr. As many mobile phones now have multimedia facilities, taking and uploading of pictures has become an activity that does not require specialist skills. Of course most SN sites offer this uploading facility but pictures may be kept for private/member viewing only.

WIKIS

A wiki is a website that uses software which can create and edit any number of interlinked pages. The most famous is Wikipedia; a free online encyclopedia which in effect is written and updated by individual users. Wikipedia contains some 6 million articles in 250 languages. It ranks highly in the top social media websites with 325 visitors per month globally. It was founded on the principle that anyone can post, edit or tweak content – a vision of a true 'for the people by the people' medium. However, more control by editors of the most popular pages has recently been introduced to boost credibility and counteract the false information and inaccuracies that appear.

Falsifying celebrity deaths is nothing new. In 1897 Mark Twain was incorrectly given an obituary that led to the famous words 'The report of my death is an exaggeration'. This preoccupation is alive and kicking for some contributors with Steve Jobs, Oprah Winfrey and Miley Cyrus all declared dead (Hattersley, 2009). Inevitably, entries logging the history, development and activities of brands and companies are common and feature highly on Google search listings. Searches for the following brands resulted in high listings for the site (shown in brackets): Innocent (3rd), Virgin Group (4th) and Mini (5th). How many corporations would prefer to hide behind their glossy brochures and sophisticated websites?

Wikis provide an excellent way of improving your internal marketing by making it easy for your staff to access information. Make sure the information is kept up to date and encourage your colleagues to contribute their success stories. It's a simple way of sharing best practice.

CITIZEN JOURNALISM AND TV

It's not just the niche media that have been invaded by CGM. News reporting and television production have both been encroached. 'Citizen journalism' has emerged as the new buccaneer of open-source news reporting. *OhmyNews*, a South Korean online newspaper, is built on the foundation that 'every citizen is a reporter' with 80 per cent of articles contributed by citizens and only 20 per cent by employed staff. It currently has about 40,000 citizen reporters in Korea. The global version, *OhmyNews International*, is published in English and has some 1,300 citizen reporters in 100 countries.

Citizen journalism is potentially akin to blogging in terms of the power wielded by the individual in reporting on their experience (my story phenomenon). Although still in a growth phase citizen journalism is likely to expand as more and more people move online for news and newspapers look to replace their diminishing advertising revenue with other sources of income.

CASE STUDY

The popularity of video in social media has also led to the production of a series of material that resembles the TV format. In 2007 the SN site Bebo launched a flagship online drama *KateModern*, based on the blog *Lonelygirl*, starring actors such as Ralf Little. Running until June 2008 it attracted an average of 1.5 million viewers per episode and involved sponsors such as Orange, Toyota and Cadbury. This was hailed as a new genre: an online soap with gripping storylines and great production.

The modest cost of online production and tools such as iMovie or Windows Movie Maker means that anyone can have a go at making a programme or even starting a TV station.

Cowboys and Indians: Burberry

Just to illustrate how CGM can contribute to the demise of a carefully crafted brand image let's consider the case of Burberry. The brand was enjoying something of a revival in the fashion world having managed to shrug off the 'landed gentry' tag and appeal to a younger, hipper crowd. Business was booming supported by the accessories range that allowed more consumers to 'buy into' the brand. And then disaster struck. 'Chavs' ambushed the brand and the famous Burberry check started to take on an altogether different meaning, flaunted on football terraces and around council estates.

There is not really a nice way to define a chav and the tabloid press had a field day reporting on chav culture. The term soon appeared in mainstream dictionaries in addition to Wikipedia. The general gist is that a chav is of working-class origin, might be unemployed or in a low-paid job and is susceptible to antisocial or aggressive behaviour. An additional dimension is the fondness of chavs for branded goods (real or fake) particularly baseball caps, polo shirts, tracksuit bottoms and anything with the Burberry check or logo. This spawned a frenzy of CGM activity that initially lampooned chavs. The current Wikipedia entry still reflects this:

Burberry is a clothing company whose products became associated with the 'chav' stereotype. Burberry's appeal to 'chav' fashion sense is a sociological example of prole drift, where an upmarket product begins to be consumed en masse by a lower socio-economic group. (en.Wikipedia.org. 2009)

An amusing cartoon video appeared on YouTube, 'Chavs in me Burberry', which to date has logged 43,398 hits and rings with the refrain 'In me Burberry, in me Burberry, I'm gonna look well smart in me Burberry'. This still lists higher on a YouTube search than any official Burberry videos.

The brand was much discussed on blogs, including ones written by so-called self-proclaimed chavs who littered their sites with Burberry references. Pictures appeared on the web, some of unsuspecting chavs in their Burberry gear, others uploaded by chavs in celebration of the chav culture as epitomized by the distinctive check. Online searches for 'Burberry' quickly picked up such sources and even now after extensive legal activity by Burberry some of this material is still easy to locate. However, the most heinous material appears to have disappeared.

That's one good thing about consumer-generated media content: it can be here today but gone tomorrow...

TOP TIPS

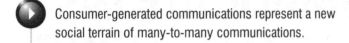 Consumer-generated communications represent a new social terrain of many-to-many communications.

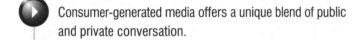 Consumer-generated media offers a unique blend of public and private conversation.

Companies are no longer in full control of brand messages.

CGM offers both threats and opportunities to brands.

CGM captures elements of popular culture that consumers are tapping into.

ACTIVITIES

Research whether your company has featured in consumer-generated media by using search engines, etc.

 Evaluate whether CGM presents a threat or an opportunity to your organization.

Consider which different CGM platforms you could use to generate positive communications for your brand/ organization.

 To get a flavour of how the user is deemed to be the driver of Web 2.0 and all things CGM look at 'Time's Person of the Year 2006: You' entry available on http://www.time.com/time/magazine/ article/0,9171,1569514,00.html.

CHAPTER 7
IMPLICATIONS FOR MANAGING COMMUNICATIONS

As communication media is changing at such a rapid rate companies need to both recognize the potential implications for their communications strategy and understand how these might be addressed. Although the Wild West might result in some shoot-outs this is not the time to resort to cowboy tactics. A systematic, planned and co-ordinated approach is needed to your communications. It is also a time for reflection and keeping a sense of perspective.

Managing communications effectively in the new frontier will require the following:

- regular monitoring and research;
- listening;
- getting off the pedestal;
- getting creative;
- honesty.

REGULAR MONITORING AND RESEARCH

In Chapter 1 we identified that communications is not a linear but a continual process. We also highlighted that you should create mechanisms for monitoring and control purposes. Sounds like hard work? Well the good news is that is has never been easier to check up on what people are saying about you and your communications, especially advertising.

Using search engines you can quickly and cheaply tap into references to your brand and organization. Although not as genuinely public as some forms of social media, the same goes for SN sites such as Facebook. Sure there have been claims of 'Big Brother' surveillance activity on SN sites and you don't want to resort to subversive tactics (see 'Honesty'). The reality is that if you really want to keep something private you don't share it via a many-to-many communications platform.

> The average number of friends on Facebook is 120 so that is potentially 14,400 people you have shared your secrets with (120 × 120). It can hardly be described as a discreet medium. The multiplier effect of SN sites and social media in general means that private becomes public very quickly. It's a bit like the relationship that some celebrities have with mainstream media channels. They need media coverage to boost their celebrity status but often see themselves as innocent victims when they attract unwanted or negative coverage as reflected in the song 'Piece of Me' by Britney Spears.

Some specifics that will help you:

- Engage in systematic scanning of the web on a regular basis, searching your brand, the competition and the market in general.

- Keep a proper record of key CGM sources even if they are not talking about your brand – they soon could be.

- Use advertising and media agencies who tend to have their fingers 'on the online pulse'. Alternatively, there's no reason why you cannot do this in-house using tools such as Google Alerts and Google Insights for Search.

- Scanning blogs is an excellent way to eavesdrop so look for ones that regularly review brands, films, etc. Miss Geeky (http://missgeeky.com) for example is followed regularly by some advertising/media practitioners. Review sites, especially if they are industry specific, such as TripAdvisor (www.TripAdvisor.co.uk) for travel, make essential browsing. Similarly, look at YouTube, especially if you or your competitors have released a new advertising campaign.

- In addition to this form of monitoring, which is fairly reactive, invite feedback from consumers, creating the opportunity for dialogue to develop. Response rates to traditional marketing research surveys is declining so create a platform that allows consumers to tell you how they feel. This can be done in many ways but you must show your hand from the outset (see 'Honesty').

- Corporate blogs can be an effective way of doing this, as can blogs written by CEOs or senior staff in a less corporate capacity; witness the number of professionals followed on Twitter. Setting up pages on SN sites such as Facebook or creating channels on CGM sites are other ways to collect feedback by engaging in dialogue.

CASE STUDY

You can always hope that satisfied consumers start their own unofficial group such as The Primark Appreciation Society, which has more than 97,000 users. The forum covers topics such as the products, staff and the store's introduction of paper carrier bags. Wisely, Primark has realized that an independent group set up in its honour is more valuable to it than a corporate attempt.

LISTENING

Patrolling the Highway is one thing but what to do with the evidence is another matter altogether. You need to first of all listen to what is being said about you. Social media presents a genuine opportunity to gauge opinion about brand equity, reputation and message effectiveness in real time. Sometimes the truth hurts, but gone are the days when chiefs could hide in the fortress of the boardroom with the latest trading figures in one hand and the *FT* in the other. In the words of Jeff Jarvis, blogging guru, the days of centralized 'we own the community, we own the brand' are over. Consumers will talk about you 'wherever they want whenever they want'.

The biggest mistake you can make is to ignore what they are saying on the basis that it only represents a few disaffected (and probably mentally unstable) outlaws staging what will turn out to be an ill-fated and derisory attempt to storm the fortress. Sure you do get a minority of obsessive people who devote themselves to brand sabotage, such as the Donovans, a father and son team, who run a gripe site about Shell (www.royaldutchshell-plc.com), which to date has published 24,000 articles about Shell. Others indulge in ranting about anything to do with marketing. But these probably do represent isolated instances.

You really need to evaluate who is writing about you, why they are writing about you and what they are saying about you. If there are more negatives than positives or many people are writing about the same problem then chances are there is a genuine issue that needs immediate investigation. It's probably a good idea at this point to take the initiative and engage in unfiltered dialogue to get to the bottom of what is really bugging consumers.

Of course, social media may also generate a good deal of positive coverage for many brands so you can identify what you are doing right and what consumers like. This will avoid making unnecessary and sometimes costly 'top down' changes – if it ain't broke don't fix it. Consumers hate to see executives meddling with brands if they are happy – it's perceived as 'not listening to us'. This does not mean you should rest on your laurels. Instead, maintain surveillance in a systematic way – bandits might be lurking around every corner.

Good creative ideas, which should enable you to enhance your brand, can come from 'listening'. For example the volume of spoof videos on YouTube present the opportunity to tap into popular culture and the minds of the young, the most hard to reach group via traditional approaches. McDonald's recently turned a consumer-generated viral video of two guys standing outside Chicago's Wrigley Field celebrating Chicken McNuggets into a 30-second spot in the United States after it attracted 1.86 million views. Unlike in the McDonald's corporation of a few years ago:

The days of command and control are gone. Today, consumers are our partners in how brands are conceived and sold.
Mary Dillon, McDonald's evp/global cmo

(Precourt, 2009)

GETTING OFF THE PEDESTAL

Let's not make any mistake about it though, social media is largely uncensored and can represent a poignantly cruel platform, characterized by a mob mentality. Witness the overweight Canadian boy who filmed himself swinging a mock light sabre as if he were a Jedi knight. Some friends placed it online and the 'Star Wars Kid' was born. Within weeks it had been viewed 900 million times. As a result of the overnight 'fame' the boy was diagnosed with depression.

Sure it can be mortifying to discover that your brand has been 'flamed' online via some defamatory material that started as a homespun jest and multiplied into a public joke/roasting/jousting/stoning, the modern-day equivalent of being in the stocks. However, a significant percentage of material contains comedy elements, especially visual material. Social media offers the path to fame in cyberspace and to be famous you need to entertain at some level.

Some hints are:

- Resist the temptation to overreact and turn it into a showdown.
- Keep a sense of perspective and indulge your sense of humour.
- Don't be precious, get off the pedestal.
- Reflect on what has happened (see 'Listening', above). What can be learned from it? Can it be harnessed in a positive way?

> Barclaycard has taken advantage of the content-creation frenzy to engage younger consumers by running a competition to produce a spoof video via YouTube of the current 'Waterslide' advert.
> First prize? A visit to the world's top waterslides!

Remember that fame in the Wild West tends to be fairly transient anyway. Every minute new material is posted, with the result that people move away quickly from yesterday's news. In addition remember that the level of exposure to social media material is highly variable – it does not mean you will encounter your own hell (see Dell Hell, page 77).

> Many spoof advertising videos never attract anywhere near the same views as the commercial advert on YouTube. Those that do tend to be clever and technically superior such as the spoof Nike advert by a group of students at Manchester Met University that made national headlines in 2006 (see also Cillit Bang on page 80 and Burberry on page 83). Don't panic because you haven't got full control over how your brand is portrayed. As long as you listen, you will be taken seriously.

GETTING CREATIVE

Creativity is not exclusive to 'creatives'! Nor is it excluded from any particular type or size of organization. Remember you're always looking to offer content AND style. To use social media effectively means forgetting the old creative and media rules and looking for fresh ways to communicate with consumers in order to really engage them. There are no hard and fast rules (apart from 'Honesty', see below). However, the most successful campaigns tend to integrate a range of media and contain an element of self-discovery.

CASE STUDY

Sony developed an award-winning digital campaign for the BRAVIA LCD TV, following the shooting of the now famous 'Balls' advert where 250,000 coloured balls were fired out of cannons down the hills of San Francisco. Sony observed from conversations taking place in the blogosphere that amateur footage of the spectacle posted on the internet had annoyed the 'Digital Influencers', an important target group.

To engender more positive conversation Sony decided not to pre-release the advert online but instead to release their own high-quality footage of the shooting of the advert in a format that could be easily viewed, linked to or downloaded by PCs, Macs and mobiles via a website (www.BRAVIA-advert.com) that linked to the original images published on Flickr. Sony also bought advertising space in relevant blogsites that referred traffic to the BRAVIA advert site, resulting in a high ranking for the site in search engines. The result was a capaign that touched the digital influencers and supported the BRAVIA brand personality of 'surprising, confident and different'.

Although it might be expected that digital companies would take advantage of social and digital media, many other types of businesses are now looking to harness the opportunity.

CASE STUDY

The PDSA, the UK's leading veterinary charity, has recently turned to social media even though supporters are generally considered to be on the elderly side. With a modest budget for communications activities, the charity now uses a range of media including Flickr, Twitter, YouTube and Facebook to encourage more people to donate time and money to the charity. Dedicated pages on Facebook managed to increase the

PDSA's supporter response rate for the London marathon by 24 per cent and the site is also used to promote 'tools' such as Your Right Pet, which helps people choose a pet to suit their circumstances.

Many SMEs with minimal budgets are also reaping the benefits by adopting creative approaches.

CASE STUDY Brewdog, a Scottish beer business, had very limited funds available when launching the brand. As local interest was lacking the founders decided to look to overseas markets such as Sweden and the United States. They sent free samples to popular bloggers in each country, which helped to convince local importers to sell and international orders took off, currently representing 80 per cent of sales. In addition, they use video to talk to customers and produced the first 'democratically designed beer' after inviting customers to vote on the best taste via video clips. So getting creative does not mean that you have to be large, digital or loaded.

INTERNAL MARKETING

Social media can also be an excellent channel for internal communications. Setting up a corporate profile on Facebook, for example, can encourage employees to actively participate in the process and share ownership. Photos can be stored here rather than on corporate systems and personal messages can be placed. Internal newsletters have often failed to be perceived as anything but top-down corporate communications. There's no doubt that your company will benefit from having a SN site, eg a Facebook page, in terms of improved relations, staff retention, recruitment, employee motivation, sharing of views, suggestions, raising awareness of new products, etc, etc.

HONESTY

There is one golden rule that should be followed in all social media activities – be honest. Honesty along with authenticity is crucial if you are to be trusted. As consumers demand more and more transparency from organizations, it is a huge mistake to underestimate their capacity to rumble a fake. Social media can transform identity but you should not use it as a means of trickery.

CASE STUDY

Remember Barry Scott of Cillit Bang fame (Chapter 6)? In 2005, just as social media was gaining momentum he emerged as a real, live person on his own blog www.barryscott. blogs.com (since withdrawn). In the spirit of all good blogs, Barry cross-referenced and cited other Cillit Bang stories posted by consumers on blogs and other social media, which helped to authenticate the fake – Barry is a totally fictitious character. He went a step too far in his desire to infiltrate the blogging community by posting a sympathetic comment on a genuine blog by Tom Coates who used the forum to talk about his estranged father. The strategy backfired with the company exposed as manipulative, callous and as abrasive as the cleaner itself.

You need to be aware that many blogs are indeed fake. The trend for Twittering celebrities has also resulted in a number of revelations that not all tweets are authentic! The *New York Times* recently outed the rapper 50 Cent as a fake Twitterer – he gets his web guru to send tweets to his 200,000 followers. Some companies, in an attempt to get in on the 'next big thing', are also paying agencies to ghost author Twitter entries. What better motivation for 'flaming'?

Any dishonest 'manipulation' of social media will eventually be exposed. In the Wild West the digital-savvy natives will outwit the chiefs eventually.

TOP TIPS

 Adopt a consistent, planned and systematic approach to using social media.

Scan the social media environment regularly and log key sources of CGM activity that might impact on your brand.

Use the opportunity to enter a dialogue with consumers.

Do not underestimate the power of social media and listen to what consumers are saying.

Do not overreact if consumers say negative things in social media.

Many different types of organization can use social media effectively and it does not necessarily require a big budget.

Creative campaigns integrate various social media channels and tend to be user-led.

If you act dishonestly you will be exposed. Authenticity and transparency are prerequisites for credibility in social media.

QUESTIONS

Before deciding how to use social media and which platforms to use you should ask the following questions (adapted from James, 2008):

 Is my brand right for social media?

 Am I using social media for the right reasons?

 How important is context?

 Are you wanted?

 How can I measure effectiveness?

There are many useful websites for you to use, such as http://www.warc.com, http://www.internetretailing.net and http://www.clickz.com. Many such sites need registration and/or fees. Remember to use your local business school as a source of research. They'll have access to these sites and more. Leeds Business School has active research programmes where staff and/or students carry out research for local companies.

Remember to look at interesting websites. The Office of Fair Trading keeps an eye on a number of companies in terms of their policies and business activities (www.oft.org).

ACTIVITIES

 Discuss how your organization could be more consumer-led in its communication activities.

 List what monitoring activities you currently do. Consider how these could be enhanced to include social media channels.

 Evaluate how your organization might react if negative stories appeared in social media.
Consider how this could be managed effectively.

CHAPTER 8
SUSTAINABILITY AND SOCIAL MEDIA MARKETING

To build relationships with your customers you must always ask yourself 'Why would clients buy from us rather than from a competitor?' One answer is that when buying goods online consumers increasingly want to buy from companies who are motivated by more than the traditional 'bottom line'. Such companies have committed themselves to acting sustainably and have adopted a 'Triple-Bottom-Line' (TBL). This is often referred to as 'People-Profit-Planet', and it's growing.

FAQ: IS SUSTAINABILITY A REAL CONCERN FOR BUSINESSES?

Many companies have flagged their green credentials via blogs, forums and SN sites. However, just saying you're 'green' isn't enough any more. Your claims will be challenged. Companies who have sought to gain from (false) environmental claims have incurred the wrath of the online community who accuse them of 'green-washing'. Simply put, companies who are not aware of the Web 2.0-driven changes in society run the risk of losing customers. So you need to respond to the new social media AND operate in increasingly sustainable ways!

Sustainability 'ownership' can be fuzzy in some companies and hotly contested in others. Some organizations recognize the importance of CSR with elements in their mission statements and may include 'green' issues (possibly a quality control issue), ethical supply policies (the purchasing department) and charitable links (all of the above!!). This corporate 'bun-fight' is partly due to differing approaches, eg what should be sustained, where and when? A way to address this is to arrange for cross-functional teams to contribute to your company's blog, wiki or SN site. Podcasts and vodcasts are very useful as your staff and other stakeholders are more likely to believe messages that come 'from the horse's mouth'. Remember, responsibility is shared between the service provider, the consumer, the community, the regulator and the government.

SUSTAINABLE MARKETING

Sustainable Marketing (SM) is predicated on the tenets of the Triple Bottom Line. Hence SM decisions should be ethical and guided by sustainable business practices which ultimately are the only way to resolve the tensions between consumers' wants and long-term interests, companies' requirements, society's long-run interests and the need for environmental balance.

This definition should act as a springboard for your company. Use it to improve your mission and vision statements. Then use SN sites, blogs and public fora to ensure that all parties are aware of your position.

Practical steps towards sustainable marketing

Third party codes of conduct can be useful in helping you to act ethically. If you're still faced with resistance from internal stakeholders you can use SN sites and blogs to share good news and suggestions from the following sources:

- The Dow Jones Sustainability Index (http://www.sustainability-index.com/);
- The FTSE4Good index (http://www.ftse.com/Indices/ FTSE4Good_Index_Series/index.jsp);
- The Global Reporting Initiative (http://www.globalreporting.org/Home).

These provide credibility to the argument for being more sustainable while acting as valuable sources of information in their own right. The FTSE4Good index, for example, includes human rights criteria. You can sell the concept of sustainability to cynics by highlighting how the public's mounting concerns are partly driven by:

- growth in prosperity;
- expansion of media coverage;
- notable disasters;
- greater scientific knowledge;
- longer term cultural shifts;
- PR and celebrity endorsement.

Most of these have increased as a direct result of the growing use of social media. With 1.7 billion internet users worldwide it's difficult to keep bad news under wraps. Celebrities are now as famous for their tweets as much as their prime activity (Stephen Fry is an honourable exception). You may argue that this is all well and good but does it really affect your business? Well, let's look at some of the implications. The following are increasing on a daily basis:

1 Levels of environmental awareness/concern leading to demand for eco-friendly products, adoption of green product substitutes, reuse/redesign/recycling of products.

2 Consumer values are shifting from consumption to conservation.

3 Demand for less pollution from industry with more conservation of resources and energy saving.

4 Greater regulation by government with businesses charged for environmental impact of their activities.

5 Demand for, and availability of, information on environmental issues with companies expected to conduct and publish ecological audits.

6 Opportunities to develop protection of the natural environment, animal rights and endangered species.

Under pressure

Pressure is increasing on companies to act sustainably. There are 1,400 environmental pressure groups in Britain alone. Any one of these could go to the press and create a bad news story for you to manage. The 13 largest green groups in the UK have over 5 million members who may exert pressure through lobbying, PR campaigns and direct action. Many activists believe that modern business practices advocate 'selling more' while 'sustainability' is about consuming less. You may need to adapt your marcomms to address stakeholders' concerns. Meet them head on by inviting them to contribute questions that you can answer – social networks are ideal for this.

CASE STUDY

Many artists have concerns regarding the use of their material on the internet and the way YouTube (who are ultimately owned by Google) has used their music. It's not a shock to realize that royalties were at the root of the problem. The songwriters formed their own websites (eg www.fairplayfor-creators.com) and SN groups to protest at the perceived lack of royalties. In 2009 Google asserted that it couldn't operate YouTube if it had to pay a royalty (no matter how small) despite the UK's independent Copyright Tribunal having established – two years earlier – that a minimum royalty per play was an essential requirement in the licensing of online services. In this case the stakeholders all have differing objectives.

Make sure you inform the local media of any good news stories that result from these dialogues. Sustainability is not simply about damage limitation; rather it's an opportunity for you to promote your good practices.

THE SUSTAINABILITY CONTINUUM

Your company must be able to position itself effectively in your market if you wish to make good decisions. Hence you must know where you're perceived to stand in terms of sustainability. One end of the sustainability continuum (Figure 8.1) represents companies who are only interested in making profit while the other represents those who are wholly concerned with the human condition and environmental protection.

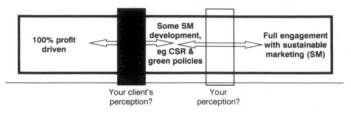

FIGURE 8.1 Sustainability continuum

Obviously such tools are limited in that companies are complex and dynamic hence the continuum can only be a snapshot. That said, it's the vital first step. Two quick questions:

1 How do you rate your company in terms of sustainability?

2 How do your customers rate your company in terms of sustainability?

If your perception is 8/10 and your customers rate you as 5/10 then you have a problem! You may be at a disadvantage – your competitors could exploit this! You need to know where you stand. If you have a poor rating you need to consider what's stopping your company from adopting sustainable SN marketing practices.

Using SN sites to overcome barriers to adopting sustainability

In future you'll probably need to operate in an increasingly sustainable fashion and you'll need to identify and remove barriers to adopting sustainability (Figure 8.2).

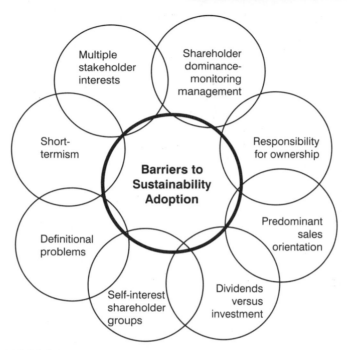

FIGURE 8.2 Barriers to sustainability adoption

You need to consider which of the barriers apply, as your organization will face challenges in moving to a more sustainable position. The CIM recognize key issues as being:

- costs;
- technical and organizational;
- conflicts between objectives;
- international implications;
- lack of visibility;
- timescale;
- lack of certainty about the nature of the problem;

- concerns regarding proposed remedies;
- tokenism;
- moral fatigue.

These can prevent adoption particularly as some issues, eg costs, can combine with others (eg timescales) to generate inertia. What's needed is a social media campaign that regularly updates your stakeholders with measurable evidence of improvements. Don't expect them to make huge leaps in the dark. Instead gently nudge them over a period of time and you'll be amazed at the progress you make. A well-established way of demonstrating progress is through benchmarking.

Benchmarking

It's a practical and proven method to help you measure your sustainability performance against your competitors. Benchmarking can also be used to instil best practice into your company across a range of issues; however, in this case we're concentrating on addressing your positioning on the sustainability continuum (Figure 8.1). The CIM defines benchmarking as a:

continuous process of measuring producers, services, and practices against strong competitors or recognized industry leaders. It is an ongoing activity that is intended to improve performance and can be applied to all facets of operation.

Benchmarking will provide the springboard for your planning as you'll need to address the issues highlighted within the benchmark report. As always, you'll have choices in how you approach this, namely, with or without external help.

Help!

Doing your own sustainability benchmarking costs you nothing but your time, although you'd be wise to read widely around the topic before you start, speak to your local business school, study a relevant course or even pay for a few hours of coaching from a professional. If you want to develop your benchmarking skills the CIM suggests the following resources:

- The Benchmark Index – formed by the DTI in 1996 and run through Business Link. Compare your businesses with others (http://www.benchmarkindex.com/).

- Best Practice Club – an organization to facilitate co-operation and information dissemination on benchmarking and best practice (http://www.bpclub.com/).

- Director's Briefing on benchmarking – quick guide to what it is, what it can mean for your organization and how to plan/implement benchmarking (http://www.bizhot.co.uk/files/St4bench.pdf).

- BuyIT – best practice network for the ICT and e-business industry. Has links to actual best practice guidelines and case studies (http://www.buyitnet.org/).

- If you want to use outside support your choices are to employ an environmental or sustainability consultant or agency. You can employ them on a one-off or ongoing basis. It should be a continuous process but you may want to test the water initially (no pun intended). Don't expect instant results as it can be a slow process. So be patient.

FAQ: So what should you benchmark?

Figure 8.3 suggests a framework that will help you to benchmark your company in terms of sustainable marketing.

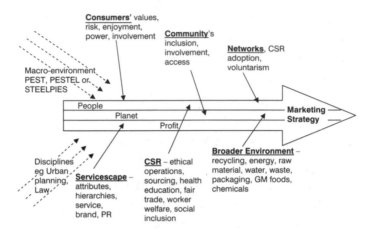

FIGURE 8.3 A framework for sustainable marketing

The factors portrayed can impact on multiple TBL elements, for example adopting a CSR policy could impact on people and profit. Most of the benchmark areas are self-explanatory. The servicescape is worth discussing briefly. Simply put, there's more to service than simply being served. Indeed the production, delivery and consumption of services revolves around how you treat customers. Every transaction represents an opportunity to show your company in a positive (or negative) light. Understanding customers' needs and having their best interest at heart sends a powerful signal. You need to measure customer satisfaction and then use SN sites and other social media to explain how you've changed in order to provide a service that's more in line with their value systems.

CASE STUDY eBay continuously seeks to address the issue of counterfeit goods for sale via its site. It constantly targets fraudulent sellers as it recognizes that its business model is based on the trust eBay buyers place in others. If this trust is misplaced and users have bad experiences, they will attribute poor marks to the seller and vicariously (via negative seller feedback) to eBay itself. Too many bad experiences could lead ultimately to the eBay business model failing. Hence it invests substantial amounts in ensuring the integrity of the items for sale. Rather than considering this as a cost it sees it as a long-term investment without which the repeat business (which ultimately underpins the eBay model) could suffer.

Once you've carried out your sustainability audit, use your social media to publish the results in a format that's easy for people to assess (Figure 8.4).

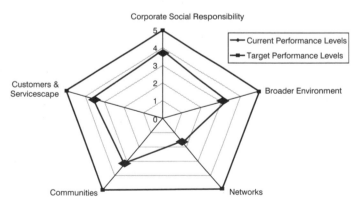

FIGURE 8.4 Sustainability polar diagram

Discuss how the measures you wish to introduce will satisfy more than one element of People-Planet-Profit. You could reduce your carbon footprint by reducing attendance at meetings and/or conferences by asking those involved to meet 'virtually' (more on this in Chapter 9). Hence these meetings could be a considerable environmental improvement undertaken at little cost. Profit is well covered elsewhere so let's consider some examples of how you can use SN sites to improve your People and Planet ratings.

PEOPLE

Sustainable marketing needs to be 'sold' on the basis of future gains and you may need to use a social media platform to improve your internal marketing in order to overcome resistance to change.

Conflicting stakeholder interests

You can use SN sites to support any proposed changes aimed at resolving stakeholder conflicts (this doesn't simply apply to sustainability!) by:

- building bases for understanding by sharing information;
- creating plans for the implementation of sustainable marketing;
- setting aside resources and making sure people are aware of your financial commitment;
- demonstrating managerial commitment;
- encouraging participation and contributions throughout the company;
- sustaining internal PR programmes and creating healthy responses to sustainability ideas.

Corporate Social Responsibility (CSR)

Are your stances on these key issues available online or merely hidden in your annual report? Do you incorporate CSR in your mission statements? Do you allude to sustainability, eg ethical supply policies or charitable links? Are your policies transparent? Are they independently audited? Where companies seek competitive advantage by abusing the reporting of their CSR practices, the reactions on SN sites is often swift and hostile!

CASE STUDY

Digital rights groups and bloggers have heaped criticism on Facebook's changed privacy policy (BBC, 2009) claiming that users were 'nudged' towards sharing updates with the wider web and made them findable via search engines. The changes (introduced in December 2009) were introduced via a pop-up and were accused of moving the settings towards 'declare everything', which some security consultants deemed to be unfair and would lead to less user control. Facebook's policy is to encourage people to be more open with their updates (ibid). This may ultimately increase traffic but could be at the expense of the user's trust being diminished.

SN sites can form the platforms for well-organized pressure groups to co-ordinate their communications efforts in order to influence corporate behaviour. You will need to monitor such sites and respond by clearly articulating your company's position. You can create a social media marcomms campaign highlighting positives from your audits as well as how you're going to implement changes where needed. Many examples exist of companies that have benefited from positive WoM by becoming increasingly sustainable.

CASE STUDY

In 2009 *Which?* magazine surveyed 15,000 banking customers to find out who were the most satisfied with their suppliers. In the resulting first annual People's Choice report the Co-operative Bank and 'smile' (their exclusively online banking outlet) were among the top three overall winners when it came to customer satisfaction. smile was awarded the highest customer score for its current account at 88 per cent, while The Co-operative Bank followed closely with 82 per cent. The highest score for savings accounts was The Co-operative Bank with 80 per cent. As a matter of interest, John Lewis (a socially responsible retailing partnership) scored the highest mark for customer satisfaction with credit cards (90 per cent). The Co-operative Bank still clearly lead the way – 17 years after its introduction in 1992 – and it is still the only UK high street bank with a customer-led ethical policy.

It could be argued that 'business' is part of the problem not the solution. On the contrary, business needs to be at the forefront of the 'sustainability' debate as trade takes place between businesses and not governments.

Sustainable marketing is an evolution of being marketing-oriented and largely uses the same frameworks and tools as conventional marketing. You will have to adapt:

- the information you use to make your decisions;
- the criteria you use to measure performance... sustainability audits may be required;
- the company values, mission and/or vision statements with which marketing objectives must fit;
- the extent to which marketing is the responsibility of the whole organization.

FIGURE 8.5 The four Ss of sustainable marketing

Figure 8.5 could act as a template where you can insert the appropriate information in order to represent your new sustainable vision statement.

Many companies have their reputations tarnished with SN-generated negative publicity of supply-side scandals with emotive issues such as child labour or 'sweatshops'. Hence with so much of business success depending on supply issues you must ensure that the stakeholders in your supply chains don't compromise how you're perceived by your online networks and communities.

Trust and voluntarism within networks

Trust can be shaped by previous experiences or co-operative efforts and on the more general reputation a firm has built up. By acting in a more sustainably responsible way you may also engender trust in consumer communities and supplier networks that can be grown through positive word-of-mouse. Hence it's logical to recognize the case for measuring and developing trust within your networks across a range of issues.

It comes down to this – to what extent can you trust the stakeholders in your network (a term preferred to supply chain) to act in ways you deem to be sustainably acceptable, eg ethically or environmentally sound? This potentially could pose a risk for your company and you need to manage the relationships carefully. Retailers, for example, are often high-profile organizations that increasingly use SN sites to seek out customer feedback.

SN and communities

You need to appreciate the importance of communities when considering marketing via SN sites. Communities are inherently based upon trust and shared values. SN sites can link various communities of stakeholders into networks. Increasingly, SN sites are used to co-ordinate differing communications campaigns of, say, ethical communities with environmental communities in campaigns, for example those opposed to the third Heathrow runway. This often happens with large political events such as the G20, Copenhagen 2009, etc, but is just as relevant to your business environment.

Larger organizations often reluctantly engage with the community. More progressive companies seek to establish relationships with the community in which it is located and develop relationships with local firms, consumers and regulators. Increasingly, SN sites are being used as a source of community feedback and you must monitor (and respond to) comments therein. Encourage satisfied customers and members of the community to contribute to your SN site. You could easily benefit from improved PR with the local community, not to mention enhancing your chances of success by favourably influencing the opinions of, say, planners who receive favourable feedback from the local community.

Ethics and SN sites

Ethical behaviour is essential in 21st century marketing and this extends to how you communicate via blogs and SN sites. To raise awareness in search engine results pages you'll seek as high a page ranking as is possible. One option is to sponsor a link via, say, Google Adwords, which will incur a charge linked to user clicks. This may be viable if your company already has an excellent reputation, USP or unusual terminology relating to your product offer.

Another factor is that the potential earnings justify the costs per click-through. It is estimated that six times as many visitors click non-sponsored sites as sponsored alternatives. Hence another practice is to leave links in the comments pages of SNs and blogs. This is known as 'link spam' and is deemed by some observers to be unethical. Indeed organizations such as Automattic provide software that 'catches' over 21 million spam comments per day. Cases have been cited where digital marketing agencies have targeted up to 500 blogs to promote their client's services.

Some argue that such 'link-building' techniques are legitimate components of search engine optimization (SEO) marketing; however, mis-information due to spam is simply another form of noise for marketers to overcome. The line between legitimate blog-commenting and blog-spamming seems blurred for too many parties and ultimately this can only lead to a breakdown of trust in your network or community. Automattic estimates that 83 per cent of all comments are spam, which is ultimately self-defeating for marketers as customers (or prospects) having to trawl through irrelevant and/or misleading information can only be deterred from engaging with SN fora or blogs.

PLANET

Increasingly, the environment will be used as a launch pad for governmental initiatives and legislation. Having a social media platform could be invaluable in terms of informing the different parties, responding to feedback and managing expectations. Recent legal changes are forcing more companies to measure and report their carbon footprint. Often, companies do this begrudgingly. More progressive companies go beyond this and undertake eco-footprinting – well worth a look online.

There is a range of excellent consulting companies such as White Young Green (http://www.wyg.com/) who will help you to environmentally benchmark your company. Many independent consultants will gladly help you, and never forget to liaise with your local business school who will also be happy to support you.

CASE STUDY

Greenscope is an environmental benchmarking tool offered by Brunel University in conjunction with retail developers. Ultimately it aims to help retailers to change consumer behaviour. It anticipates a retailer's move to a green marketing strategy is likely to take up to five years to complete and its approach is based on detailed consultations.

ML Sun offers eight tips to get you started on an environmentally sustainable marketing plan:

1 Become fluent in sustainability – understand how it relates specifically to your product or service – if you aren't aware, your customers won't be either.

2 Educate your customers – show the practical value and benefits of what is being offered and why it's worth a higher price.

3 Use clear language that conveys a positive image of your product or service.

4 Be wary of sending contradictory messages and 'green washing'. Are you advertising your company as 'green' with little to back it up? Are you endorsing environmental causes merely to boost your company image? If so, you're likely to be found out.

5 Highlight environmental progress and programmes your company has in the works. Companies of all sizes have become popular models of corporate excellence for the environmental/sustainability initiatives they have in place.

6 Invite consumers into the dialogue – ask for their feedback and not just on the product but on how you serve them. Consumers want to know whether you're socially responsible too.

7 Network with other green-based businesses. Green business alliances are being established and are becoming certified as green by entities such as the American Consumer Council.

8 Green it if you mean it. Offer the best product available because it makes sense and if you want everyone to benefit in the long term.

And finally...

Sustainability is a challenge that you'll face over the next 30–40 years. It isn't going away! Your mission, should you choose to accept it, is to be an agent of change and embrace the need to grow your companies profitably AND sustainably. It's not whimsy or ethereal – rather it's about the nuts and bolts of business. Happy customers spend more and are more loyal. Customers will increasingly be concerned about sustainability, and satisfying their green and ethical concerns will go some way towards a guarantee of long-term success.

TOP TIPS

 Buying is always guided by consumers' thoughts, feelings and actions and since we take on attitudes, beliefs, opinions and values of others, companies who are not aware of changes in society run the risk of alienating customers.

 All companies have 'sustainability' responsibilities. You need to ensure that your brand is well represented on SN sites and other social media in terms of how you take responsibility and exceed all expectations. Also use SN sites to clarify the roles of consumers, online communities, regulators and the politicians!

 All companies are located on the sustainability continuum and need to be aware of their position in order to be able to position (or reposition) themselves within their markets by making effective strategic and operational decisions.

You will need to look towards operating in an increasingly sustainable fashion. Hence you may need to benchmark your current performance and identify (and remove) barriers to adopting sustainability.

 Ensure you regularly monitor SN sites and other user-generated media. Then make any necessary changes and communicate your reactions with the online communities and networks.

QUESTIONS

 What are the key benefits that an organization can attain by adopting sustainable marketing practices?

 Many organizations struggle to adopt the changes needed to be more sustainable – what could these barriers be? How is this reflected in your company?

 How would you go about identifying your position on the sustainability continuum or benchmarking your company in terms of sustainability?

ACTIVITIES

There's precious little on sustainable marketing even in the key marketing texts. To look at a range of academic conference papers (which cover a large range of industries around the world) look at: The Corporate Responsibility Research Conference website http://crrconference.org/.

The following book contains a number of informative studies on sustainability including key sustainability: Starkey, R and Welford, R (2001) *The Earthscan Reader in Business and Sustainable Development*, Earthscan Publishing: London.

The 'Inside CRM' site provides an opportunity to differentiate between link-spam and legitimate blogs. It offers a comprehensive list of Facebook tips that techies will love as it goes into great detail; however, the real challenge is looking at the postings and deciding which of the contributors have included links to their sites. You decide (which is spam) in this case and then consider how you may want to control this on your site.

Have a look at ML Sun's suggestions for green marketing at http://maeleesun.com/2008/08/22/green-marketing-8-tips-to-get-you-started-on-an-environmentally-sustainable-marketing-plan/.

CHAPTER 9
LOOKING TO THE FUTURE

Digital media presents a fast paced and dynamic communications environment. It is difficult to predict to what extent exactly our media consumption habits will change irrevocably in the future. However, we are already reading less hard-copy newspapers, preferring to get our news online, and our television viewing habits are changing with more viewing 'on demand' options. Multimedia mobile phones are also giving us the opportunity to use a variety of media via a hand-held, portable device, which frees us from some of the conventions that have been associated with consumption of traditional media. There has been a gradual shift in advertising expenditure from print and TV to internet channels, to the extent that in 2009 online expenditure overtook TV for the first time. So what does the future hold?

VIRTUAL WORLDS

There is a growing trend for people to turn to alternative forms of entertainment such as virtual worlds. These are interactive simulated environments accessed by multiple users through an online interface, often in 3D. They offer users an alternative reality where they can escape their ordinary lives and participate in a fantasy world. However, the world continues regardless of whether individual users are logged in. Most worlds allow you to create an 'avatar', a computerized version of yourself that engages in role play within the world. You decide your sex, your name, your physical build or appearance and your clothing.

Virtual worlds allow members to alter, develop, build or submit customized content, hence they share characteristics of CGM. For example in addition to avatar creation you can decorate and furnish a virtual apartment. Worlds also allow and encourage SN activity such as forming relationships, social groups, communities, etc. Below is a table listing just a few of the worlds by category (adapted from www.virtualworldsreview.com).

TABLE 9.1 List of virtual worlds by category

Kids	Teens
Club Penguin	Dubit
Disney's Toontown	Habbo Hotel
Whyville	There
Virtual Magic Kingdom	The Sims Online
	Coke Studios

20s–30s	40+
The Manor	Traveler
Second Life	Voodoo Chat
Cybertown	Moove
Virtual Ibiza	VP Chat
The Pal	

The amount of uptake increases with every generation. The vast majority of grade 5 (ie 10-year-old) children are online virtually via sites such as Roblox and Club Penguin.

When they replace the current generation of university undergraduates they'll have experienced virtual reality for 10 years, many with multiple avatars. Then they'll go into industry and will think nothing of holding meetings virtually. Hence the scope of virtual worlds is vast; here are some ways they can be used to support marketing communications:

Buy space (land) in the world

Second Life allows organizations to buy space or islands in the world and establish an interactive presence. A range of organizations including BBC, IBM, Reebok and Warner Bros have done this in addition to a number of educational institutions. Recently, the law firm Field Fisher and Waterhouse opened an office here.

Product placement

Pay to feature your brand or organization in a world, such as a poster for Diesel in the underground in *Dubit*.

Sponsor a promotion

Run a competition or other sales promotion activity in a world. For example, pop-tarts sponsored a competition in *Habbo Hotel*.

Create a branded world

Coke Studios is a world that has been designed to promote the brand by creating personal connection with consumers via a sponsored community. This can generate co-branding opportunities such as the Wal-Mart room in *Coke Studios*.

Selling products or services

Avatar creation can involve customizing your appearance. For example, you can buy and customize a pair of Reebok trainers for your avatar to wear in *Second Life*. Some worlds, such as *There*, offer members the opportunity to design and create their own product ranges, which could involve partnerships with brands. Increasingly, paid services such as relationship counselling, wedding planning and legal services are in demand.

Video games

An alternative communications platform is offered by video games, which offer brands the opportunity for advertising and product placement. These are starting to attract the eyeballs of big advertisers. Advertising can be woven into the game and contextualized in order to avoid resistance from gamers and some are interactive. Popular game titles include *Thief*, *Super Mario*, *Ferrari Challenge*, *Bratz*, *PKR Poker* and *Quake*. In addition there are advergames – games made for the purpose of promoting a brand or product such as *Mad Mix* (Pepsi) and *Avoid the Noid* (Domino's Pizza).

There are three major types of branding opportunities:

- Monopolization occurs in advergames where the brand totally dominates a game.

- Billboarding allows brands to occur 'naturally' and in the context of the game's environment (ie hoardings, flyers, stadium ads). Such ads can be static (ie one-off messages), dynamic (such as the moving ads around football pitches) or interactive.

- Utilization is a more involved approach where the characters in the game use products in a natural way. For example, in a car racing game the pit crews may use Castrol motor oil.

THE NEW HYBRIDS

The difference between virtual worlds, games and SN sites can sometimes be blurred and as social media further evolves this is increasingly likely to be the case.

CASE STUDY

Sony released *Home* as a free 'game' on the PlayStation 3 console. It represents a form of virtual world in which you can create an avatar, decorate your virtual apartment (a Ligne Roset sofa would cost £1.59), invite virtual friends round to chat/hang out and take a trip to the virtual mall. Other brands signed up to the site include Red Bull, Audi, Diesel and Snickers. Users spent £700,000 on items in the first month. *Home* requires less technical expertise than, say, *Second Life* – a 'hardcore' world – but also offers more than Facebook, as networking is accompanied by moving pictures.

World of Warcraft, a huge platform with 11.5 million subscribers, is described as a multiplayer online role-playing game. It involves aspects of virtual worlds, gaming and social networking.

So in the future, as social media mutates and reshapes, it might be less about individual channels and more about the overall landscape or the long media tail, as it has been described.

VIRAL CAMPAIGNS

As discussed in Chapter 5, we're starting to witness the impact of the 'viral' campaign on marketing communications. Viral marketing is a potent form of communication that (being an unpaid form of many-to-many communication) can be particularly useful for SMEs, entrepreneurs, charities and other organizations with smaller marcomms budgets.

Viral campaigns may be deliberately emotive and provocative as they seek a reaction from users that can be as simple as passing the message on. They:

- often seek to target networks and communities that have the size or importance for the viral message to cross over to the traditional mass media;
- use a range of media to rapidly spread a message from one person to another, thereby creating a 'buzz' effect;
- are particularly effective when supported by digital media channels due to their interactive and instant nature;
- can be particularly effective in reaching younger consumers as they chime with many of their fundamental psychological, social and cultural needs.

Such campaigns fuel consumer-to-consumer interactions enabling consumers to discover and/or to be involved in the campaign. This is an antidote to corporately controlled campaigns based on traditional 'lean back' channels. Using the digital lean forward channels, organizations can engage existing and potential customers in campaigns that make them feel empowered, rather than manipulated. Brands stand a much better chance of 'getting under the radar' if they have consumers on board. It comes back to the partnership ethos discussed earlier.

One way to easily create viral activity is to integrate channels wherever possible by creating links. Many platforms offer the facility to link to others. You also need to identify the platforms that are key to your target market in order to upload your material where it will count.

Viral video seeding is a planned strategy that aims to result in a video or series of videos going viral. You might need help here. The London-based agency Unruly Media, for example, pitches itself as the world's leading exponent of viral video marketing. It helps global agencies and brands to promote viral videos and other forms of branded content on YouTube, Facebook, Twitter, influential blogs, cult websites and social media applications.

CASE STUDY

A classic viral campaign was for the Batman movie *The Dark Knight*. The audience was positioned as full-blood interactive partners in the campaign, which involved a range of channels including a string of websites, e-mails, blogs, YouTube and mobile phones along with ambient media vehicles. Fans were empowered to create a Batman universe for themselves by engaging in activities such as voting, signing petitions, role play and video and picture creation. The results were outstanding, with high recorded levels of consumer activity and content creation leading to buzz and a high 'likeability' factor.

WHAT ABOUT THE MESSAGE?

At this juncture it's worth revisiting the notion of the 'message' (see Chapter 1). All digital channels are subject to the same noise problems as traditional media (Figure 1.1) so development of the message is no less important. You still need to start with the story. There is no point getting carried away with the variety of new and exciting channels if the message does not deliver. You need to consider whether consumers will be prepared to spend time on the content and assess its 'stickiness' factor. Remember, you are no longer in control!

The higher the 'talkability' factor, the more likely people will be to engage and pass on to others. So creativity will remain at the heart of a good campaign. Agencies will continue to play a pivotal role in campaign development as they adapt and adjust to the challenges and opportunities of social media. The threat that agencies will be disintermediated by technologists (the archetypal '12-year-olds in a garage') will recede as they regroup and respond to client needs (Grande, 2009). However, it is inevitable that skills offered by 'new media' agencies such as Unruly Media will be very much in demand.

REGULATION

So far in the Wild West, freewheeling anarchy has flourished. However, as communications expenditure continues to shift from the confines of traditional media we will see more regulatory activity in social media. This activity is likely to cover disclosure of interest, codes of practice, protection of minors and offensive material. However, we are unlikely to see the restrictions on amount of exposure to commercial messages that we see in commercial TV. Just how easy it will be to police channels is debatable, so self-regulation is likely to be a key dimension.

TOP TIPS

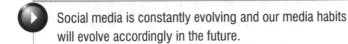 Social media is constantly evolving and our media habits will evolve accordingly in the future.

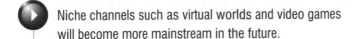 Niche channels such as virtual worlds and video games will become more mainstream in the future.

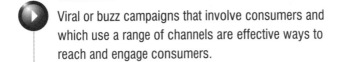 Viral or buzz campaigns that involve consumers and which use a range of channels are effective ways to reach and engage consumers.

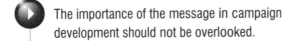 The importance of the message in campaign development should not be overlooked.

 Agencies will continue to provide key services to clients.

 More attention will be given to the regulation of social media.

ACTIVITIES

 Consider how you could create a viral campaign for your organization.

Research the virtual world *Second Life*. How could your organization use this as a communications tool?

Select two social media channels. How might these be subject to regulation in the future?

Have a look at some relevant websites. Start with Unrulymedia http://www.unrulymedia.com [accessed 10 June 2009] and http://www.virtualworldsreview.com [accessed 17 February 2009].

CHAPTER 10
QUESTIONS ANSWERED

This chapter is designed to provide answers for chapter-related questions and also to provide suggestions of further reading materials to add breadth and depth.

CHAPTER 1: A CHANGING LANDSCAPE

Answers to questions

1 Encoding refers to dressing the message with signs, symbols and language that the target receiver can interpret and understand. Decoding refers to this process of understanding the encoded message. Noise is the clutter or information overload that occurs every day and has the potential to distort the communication process and the message being received.

2 Experts or 'opinion formers' are often used in forms of communication as they can be deemed to lend a degree of credibility to the brand, product and message.

3 The key difference between an opinion leader and an opinion former is that opinion formers, due to their education and/or profession, are deemed to be experts in their field, whereas opinion leaders tend to be from the same peer or reference group and are influential because of their social standing.

References

Brand Republic (2009) article from www.brandrepublic.com

Fill, C (2009) *Marketing Communications: Interactivity, communities and content*, 5th edn, Financial Times

Hemsley, S (2008) Networking for business, *Precision Marketing*, **20** (12), pp 19–20

CHAPTER 2: THE ENVIRONMENTS

Help with activities

1 The PEST factors constitute the key forces in the macro environment: political, economic, social-cultural and technological factors. Other variables in the macro environment include economic, environmental, legal, political, informational, ethical/educational, sustainable. The most common acronyms are PEST, PESTEL (the CIM's preferred option), STEEPLE, EPISTLE, STEEPLE, STEELPIES (Neil's preferred option).

2 The monitoring of the environments is very much dependent upon the nature of the industry and markets you see yourself operating in. Ideally, you should be monitoring the environments daily, even in a stable climate. The macro environment is turbulent and dynamic – anything can happen! To monitor the macro environment read quality newspapers and check out the BBC website on a regular basis (www.bbc.co.uk). Also, central and local government publishes an enormous amount of data regarding social trends, economic data, etc. Trade bodies can also provide key data (eg the British Retails Consortium via www.brc.org.uk). Reading magazines/books/articles such as *The Economist* (www.economist.com) is also helpful.

3   The micro environment is partly controllable and influenced due to the relationships that the organization has with the relevant parties, namely customers, competitors, suppliers, distributors, owners, staff, managers, directors, agents, wholesalers, retailers, facilitators and publics such as communities.

Reference

ABI research (2008) The Mobile Browser Market, http://www. abiresearch.com/products/market_research/MCCS [accessed 14 December 2008]

CHAPTER 3: USERS AND/OR CUSTOMERS?

Answers to questions

1   You'll need to adjust to the new reality where you won't be able to identify your prospects, customers and/or consumers. This makes your data management considerably tougher, for example which info would you enter on a marketing

information system such as a database? Also people tend to lack self-criticism online while being overly (and overtly) critical of service failures. Hence you'll need to decode the messages reaped from SN sites in order to ascertain the strength of feeling. Much of the secondary information is based on fabrication of identities with some users having multiple identities. Attempts to force the SN users to provide more identification can be problematic, as Facebook recently found out. Still, it's worth selling the notion of community and the more they share with you the greater the sense of community could be.

2 Different stakeholders have different levels of interest, willingness to react and power. You need to map the stakeholders and then tailor your internal comms mix to optimize your efficiency. Make information freely available in order to satisfy gatekeepers. Seek input from your staff and then use their data to create FAQs in order to win over influencers and deciders. Encourage users to provide marks (out of 10) for internal services. The resulting gap analysis can only improve your company. Finally, improve your internal marketing; you need to promote the concept of internal customers even if the transactional element is only notional.

3 The information search and evaluation stages have been revolutionized by the advent of SN sites. It's no longer about closing deals. Nowadays it's about nudging the customer by managing the information they're seeking. Prospects now use price comparison and SN sites as a matter of routine. You need to monitor how your goods are perceived and adjust your comms mix to aid the user's decision making.

References

Chaffey (2010) http://www.davechaffey.com/

EIAA (2009) European Interactive Advertising Association website. Online article: Media Multi-taskers: More Engaged & Entertained Online. http://www.eiaa.net/news/eiaa-articles-details.asp?lang=1&id=203 [accessed 16 June 2009]

Fill, C (2009) *Marketing Communications: Interactivity, communities and content*, 5th edn, Financial Times

Fraser, M and Dutter, S (2008) *Throwing Sheep in the Boardroom: How online social networking will transform your life, work and world*, Wiley

CHAPTER 4: BUILDING RELATIONSHIPS

Answers to questions

1 First you should embrace the idea of engaging with your SN audience. At times things will undoubtedly go wrong and your reaction says much more about your company than when things are proceeding smoothly. Remember you never win an argument with customers so you must recognize why they've posted negative feedback. Take responsibility or, as some say, ownership. Address the underlying causes and then invite the SN users to comment on the improved services. Most people are fundamentally decent and they'd struggle to be critical of a company that apologized and then was seen to take corrective measures.

2 All companies can benefit from having a better appreciation of the benefits their customers are seeking... so ask them. Use the 'what if' approach adopted by companies such as Tesco. It's not a coincidence that they've gone from being merely a greengrocer in the 1970s to being one of the world's leading retailers. They've used their Club card as a mechanism to ask 'what if we offered...?'. This simple act has driven their product diversification.

3 You're looking to move your communications from being erratic to continuous so have a flow of good news to give them – report your achievements. Ensure the focus is on benefits and not features, eg relate value for money rather than price. Think long term – make your comms reflect this while stressing your emphasis on customer service. Dissatisfied customers have limited commitment, hence your aim is to shift your customer expectations to 'high'. This way you can differentiate yourself from your competitors. Use internal marketing and get contributions from all staff – not just the customer-facing ones. Co-ordinate your use of SN sites, comparison websites and public fora.

References

Chaffey (2010) http://www.davechaffey.com/

Da Silva, R (2008) Online brand attributes and online corporate brand images, *European Journal of Marketing*, **42** (9/10), pp 1039–58

Piercy, N F (2009) *Market-led Strategic Change: Transforming the process of going to market*, 4th edn, Butterworth Heinemann

Reid-Smith, E (2009) Seven-step e-Loyalty Consulting Process (http://www.e-loyalty.com)

The Times (2009) Social network sites offer a new opportunity for retailers, 20 April, online article, http://business.timesonline.co.uk/tol/business/industry_sectors/retailing/article6128182.ece [accessed 8 March 2010]

CHAPTER 5: THE MARKETING COMMUNICATIONS MIX

Answers to questions

1 Advantages of advertising include the ability to communicate on a mass scale if used with the correct media. Complex messages can be created and products and services demonstrated if, again, the correct media is used. It can be a cost-effective tool, particularly in terms of SN. Disadvantages of advertising include its ability to be used in an unethical manner. It can be a persuasive tool and therefore can be deemed to be manipulative if used inappropriately. Until fairly recently it has always been a non-personal communication tool. However, with the advent of digital media, strides have been taken to overcome aspects of this drawback. Advertising also has the reputation of being expensive.

2 Effective sales promotional activities in the B2C market include: BOGOF, competitions, free prize draws, free products through redemption.

3 Viral marketing is 'the unpaid peer-to-peer communication of often provocative content originating from an identified sponsor using the internet to persuade or influence an audience to pass along the content to others.'
(Baines, Fill, Page, 2008: 849).

References

Baines, P, Fill, C and Page, K (2008) *Marketing*, Oxford University Press

Bearne, S (2008) *Half of UK internet users claim to have never clicked on a banner ad*, New Media Age

Cruz and Fill (2008) Evaluating viral marketing: isolating the key criteria, *Marketing Intelligence & Planning*, **26** (17), pp 743–58

Digital PR, *PR Week*, 28 November 2008

CHAPTER 6: CONSUMER-GENERATED MEDIA

Help with activities

1 A Google search on company name will quickly identify if anyone is talking about you. However, you may need to spend time trawling through the pages. Do not assume that a listing will be on the first page. If there have been any issues/problems recently at the organization, use these as search words.

2 Your evaluation might be along the following lines:

CGM as a threat – negative word of mouth/mouse, undermining of brand/corporate communication efforts, changing the perception of hitherto loyal customers, can be time-consuming to monitor, difficulties of managing CGM.

CGM as an opportunity – positive word of mouth/mouse, connect with customers, generate direct and cost-effective feedback, source of idea generation, build up following of advocates.

3 Consider a range of platforms and allocate some time to exploring them. If you need to join to get access then join. Look at how other companies are using the sites. Is it effective? Could you adapt this? Also think about how you could link activity on more than one site, as aggregation and integration will intensify your efforts.

References

Barras, C (2009) Gallery: Flickr users make accidental maps, http://www.newscientist.com 27 April 2009 [accessed 20 July 2009]

Hattersley, G (2009) The wiki-snobs are taking over, *The Sunday Times*, News Review section, 8 February 2009, p 6

Poynter, R and Lawrence, G (2007) Insight 2.0: new media, new rules, new insight, ESOMAR Annual Congress, Berlin, September 2007

Redfern, P (2009) Analysis of Flickr photos could lead to online travel books, http://www.news.cornell.edu, 28 April 2009 [accessed 5 June 2009]

Snol, L (2009) Consumer generated media gains trust, http://www.infoworld.com, 8 July 2009 [accessed 20 July 2009]

Wikipedia (2009) http://en.wikipedia.org/wiki/Chavs [accessed 20 June 2009]

CHAPTER 7: IMPLICATIONS FOR MANAGING COMMUNICATIONS

Help with activities

1 To help you answer this, rate how customer-led your organization is on a scale of 1–10. Now rate how customer-led your communications are. Less than five means that you have quite a long way to go. Ideas for involving customers more include: introducing an element of interactivity or response in your communications; giving customers the opportunity to give feedback; asking customers to create some communications, such as an advert; running competitions to appear in adverts. Some of these involve using your own website more effectively.

2 Regular monitoring might involve using sources such as newspapers, business and trade press, talking to

suppliers, distributors, retailers, customers and maybe even competitors, getting field intelligence from the sales force, using traditional market research techniques and buying research reports and subscribing to relevant research services such as Mintel or Retail Audits. You will need to identify who currently undertakes monitoring activity and when. Do you have a dedicated research function or is it absorbed into general marketing activities? Is it undertaken systematically or on an ad hoc basis? Then consider how to incorporate monitoring of social media into your existing system. Do the people responsible have the technical skills? Will any training be necessary? You will need to list the social media sources that may be relevant to your organization. Even if you are not featured, regular monitoring will give a good insight into what customers are talking about or engaging with and who are the influencers.

3 It might be easier here to imagine a negative story that feasibly could appear about your organization. Typical reactions might include outrage, panic, annoyance, arrogance, denial, cover up, irrationality, over-compensating the disgruntled and initiating an internal witch-hunt to identify who should be held responsible. This could be managed more effectively by firstly assessing the potential damage – is this just an isolated story or has it reached a community? Then you should look at the nature of the complaint or source of the story – is it about product malfunction or staff/service issues? Product malfunctions are probably easier to address immediately. Staff and service issues take longer to address and may be a symptom of the organizational culture. This can be used as an opportunity for an organization to critically and honestly review its operations. Finally, you must decide on what action, if any, to take. You will need to be proactive and respond in a transparent way.

Answers to questions

1 There should be a match between the fundamental values of your brand and the context of the social media environment.

2 There should be a true role for your social media activity within your total communications strategy. Don't just use it to be seen there or because your competition are there.

3 For example, if using advertising on SN sites are you happy for your brand to sit alongside profile page images of last night's heavy partying?

4 Brand messages can be intrusive. Disrupting social networking activity might be counter-productive.

5 Currently there is no consistency of measurement across each social media channel. Make sure that the possible implications are understood.

References

James, L (2008) 'Should you advertise on social networking sites?', WARC Best Practice, http://www.warc.com [accessed 2 December 2009]

Precourt, G (2009) AMA Mplanet 2009: McDonald's global brand promise and the branding of customers, http://www.warc.com [accessed 4 April 2009]

CHAPTER 8: SUSTAINABILITY AND SOCIAL NETWORK MARKETING

Answers to questions

1   Customers are increasingly concerned about the TBL elements of sustainability. Having a better fit with consumers can only lead to increased customer satisfaction. The use of SN sites will provide crucial feedback, which in turn will improve your chances of getting it right first time. Ultimately this is good for turnover, bottom line and market share. By dealing with happier customers your staff will be more satisfied and hence more productive with less attrition and higher motivation. Sustainable marketing and marketing orientation go hand in hand and share many of the same benefits.

2   Some stakeholders will act as gatekeepers and will resist the investment needed to make your company more sustainable. They'll denigrate sustainability by suggesting it's fluffy or whimsical despite the evidence to the contrary. Use exemplars of good practice – point them towards the Co-operative's CSR platform – it's as good as any in the world. It's transparent, independently audited and they refuse to take business that contradicts their ethical policies. Over 160 years of success and growth can't be all wrong!

3   Remember that customers should be at the heart of all of your business and marketing decisions and activities. Your company needs to be both inward and externally focused to truly understand and react to changing customer needs and trends such as

sustainability. Researching who your customer is and what they require is a start to developing a relationship with them. You could use one of the increasing numbers of ethical/green consultancies to help you benchmark – indeed the first attempt will usually benefit from independence. Alternatively contact your local business school – all of whom teach ethics and would be happy to help you by providing a team of business students to help with your research.

Reference

BBC (2009) Facebook faces criticism on privacy change. Online article downloaded from http://news.bbc.co.uk [accessed 12 December 2009]

CHAPTER 9: LOOKING TO THE FUTURE

Help with activities

1 First of all you need to identify a theme. Nobody will pass on mainstream company-generated communications (unless it is really bad or really funny, or both!). What would get people engaged? Then you need to think of which social media platforms your current and potential customers might use and how these might connect with each other. If you are struggling then start with an e-mail. What would customers pass on to their friends?

2 Read about *Second Life* first from other sources via Google. Then look at the site and if possible join to

get a real feel for this medium. If you bought some land, what could you do with it? Open a shop, open up an office to sell services, give a factory tour, create a demonstration lab, conduct focus groups? Look at what other companies have done to get some ideas.

3 Regulation will depend on the channel but areas might include guarding privacy, agreeing to terms and conditions about use of information, limiting the number of adverts, protecting minors, authenticating sponsored activity, codes of practice, introduction of censorship/screening and creation of watchdog bodies.

To consider improving your networking check out the business network site http://www.linkedin.com/.

Reference

Grande, C (2009) Social media's emerging communications model, WARC Online Exclusive http://www.warc.com [accessed 17 February 2009]

Virtual Worlds Review (2009) http://www.virtualworldsreview.com/info/categories.shtml [accessed 20 June 2009]

GLOSSARY

advergame A video game that is designed primarily to advertise a product, organization or viewpoint.

advertising A non-personal form of communicating a message that uses paid-for media to reach the intended target receivers.

AIDA model of communication A communication model that aims to obtain Attention, Interest, Desire and Action.

ASA Advertising Standards Authority is the independent body set up to regulate advertising and other forms of marketing communication.

avatar A computer user's representation of himself/herself. An avatar can be three-dimensional as in games and virtual worlds; two-dimensional as in pictures on SN sites; or text-based as in chat rooms.

banner ad An image on a website used to advertise a product or service.

benefit The gain obtained from the use of a particular product or service. Consumers purchase product/services because of their desire to gain these built-in benefits.

blog A frequently updated diary/journal for public consumption.

blogosphere Sum total of all blogs and their interconnections. The term implies that blogs exist together as a connected community via which everyday authors can publish their opinion.

brand equity The value of a brand.

brand extension strategy The process of using an existing brand name to extend on to a new product/service, eg the application of the brand name Virgin on a number of business activities.

brand name Used for the identification of goods or services. Can be a name, term, sign or symbol. A well-managed brand should uphold certain values and beliefs.

brand repositioning An attempt to change consumer perceptions of a particular brand. For example, VW has successfully repositioned the Skoda brand.

break-even A point for a business where turnover is equivalent to all costs.

buzz marketing Word-of-mouth communications between consumers that can be delivered or enhanced by the network effects of the internet.

CIPR Chartered Institute of Public Relations – the largest professional body of PR in Europe.

citizen journalism Where members of the public play an active role in the collection, reporting, analysis and dissemination of news and information. Also known as public or street journalism.

competitive advantage Offering a different benefit from that of your competitors.

consumer-generated media General activity on the web where consumers contribute their own content. Also known as user-generated content.

data mining Application of artificial intelligence to solve marketing problems and aiding forecasting and prediction of marketing data.

decoding The interpretation of an encoded message by the target receivers.

direct marketing The process of sending promotion material to a named person within an organization.

diversification A growth strategy that involves an organization to provide new products or services. The new products on offer could be related or unrelated to the organization's core activities.

e-marketing The marketing side of e-commerce. Features efforts to market and sell products and services over the internet.

encoding The dressing of a message with signs, symbols and language the target receiver can interpret and understand.

flaming A popular pastime online. A flame is a hostile and insulting message posted online or e-mailed.

flash mobbing The sudden gathering of a large group of people in a predetermined location to perform some brief action then disperse quickly. The term is generally only applied to gatherings organized via viral e-mails, SN sites or telecommunications. It is not applied to publicity stunts organized by PR agencies.

focus group A simultaneous interview conducted among six to eight respondents. The aim is to obtain qualitative information on the given topic.

lean back channels Term used to describe communication channels where the consumer plays a passive role. Television has traditionally been a lean back channel.

lean forward channels Term used to describe communication channels where the consumer plays an active role. The internet is a classic lean forward channel.

long media tail Represents the shape of the media curve that begins with traditional mass media channels with high reach, such as television, and flattens out with expanding channels, such as SN sites and blogs which have lower reach.

macro environment The uncontrollable forces external to an organization. The acronym STEEL PIES can be used to highlight the external forces at play.

market position The perception of a product or an organization from the view of the consumer.

market research Analysing and collecting data on the environment, customers and competitors for purposes of business decision making.

marketing mix The strategy of the organization consisting of products, price, place and promotion strategy (also known as the four Ps).

marketing planning A written document that plans the marketing activities of an organization for a given period. The document should include an environmental analysis, marketing mix strategies and any contingency plans should an organization not reach its given objectives.

mash up Original material such as a video or an advert that is edited from more than one source to appear as one.

media The vehicle through which a message is transported to the target receiver.

micro environment A uniquely configured environment that surrounds the immediate organization. The micro environmental forces include: customers, suppliers, distributors, competitors, publics.

niche marketing The process of concentrating your resources and efforts on one particular segment.

noise Any distraction to the communication process, eg daily distractions, moods.

OFCOM Office of Communication – the communications regulator.

opinion former A person who through their professional expertise has influence upon others.

opinion leader A person who through their social standing has the ability to influence others.

personal selling Selling a product or services one-to-one.

pop up An ad that appears in a window on top of the browser window in a website.

primary data The process of organizing and collecting data for an organization.

product cannibalization Losing sales of a product to another similar product within the same product line.

product life cycle The life stage of a product; includes introduction, growth, maturity and decline.

public relations The process of building good relations with the organization's various stakeholders.

receiver The intended target market.

relationship marketing Creating a long-term relationship with existing customers. The aim is to build strong consumer loyalty.

reverse marketing Encouraging the customer to seek the company/brand rather than the marketer seeking the customer.

sales promotion An incentive to encourage the sale of a product/service, eg money-off coupons; buy one, get one free.

search engines A database of many web pages which then 'ranks' the results of a search term.

secondary data Researching information that has already been published.

segmentation The process of dividing a market into groups that display similar behaviour and characteristics.

sender The person or body that sends a message to an intended target receiver.

stickiness Using content on the internet to encourage users to spend longer on a site, visit the site more often or give more attention to the site.

SWOT analysis A model used to conduct a self-appraisal of an organization. The model looks at internal strengths and weaknesses and external environmental opportunities and threats.

test marketing Testing a new product or service within a specific region before national launch.

viral marketing The use of pre-existing social network sites by marketers to spread brand messages and other related marketing content. It is derived from the self-replicating nature of computer viruses.

viral video seeding Strategic and targeted plan of activity that results in a video or series of videos going viral. This usually involves identifying communities that fit the brand and then uploading the video across multiple platforms with the aim that it will be spread to like-minded people.

virtual world A computer-based, simulated environment that users can inhabit and interact with via avatars.

widgets Applications or 'gizmos' that help display and present information.

wiki Software that allows the co-creation and contribution of knowledge on a particular topic by groups of people. Allows contribution and collaboration from a number of users.

word-of-mouth Consumers pass on information, opinions and feedback about brands and companies. Typically a consumer tells 5 or 10 friends and then the communication fades. This is different to viral marketing where the communication spreads. Word-of-mouse is similar but is transmitted via an internet-based platform.